Praise for Using Lead Management on Purpose

"I learned a lot of choice theory when I read it. It is clear and concise on principles and practices. I read it in one day and really enjoyed it—it's a great book!"

—**Dr. William Glasser, MD,** author of *Choice Theory: A New Psychology of Personal Freedom*

"The use of 'fairy tale as truth' frees the imagination from restraints and provides business organizations with a framework of successful strategies that lead to the cutting edge of quality products and competitiveness on the world stage. A must-read for systems-minded leadership!"

—**Jean Seville Suffield**, Choice-Makers, International Trainer and Author

USING LEAD MANAGEMENT ON
PURPOSE

Other Works by Ken Pierce as Contributing Author:

The Child in the Curriculum—Child Care and Education, Canadian Dimensions—1990

DACUM Manual—1995.

A Useful Approach to Facilitating Individual Adjustment to Organizational Change—The Competency Casebook—1998

Foundations of Early Childhood Education—2006

The Dance of Bullying—A New Look—2007 (In Press)

USING LEAD MANAGEMENT ON PURPOSE

PURPOSE

CREATING EXCELLENT PRODUCTS AND SERVICES FOR A GLOBAL ECONOMY

Kenneth L. Pierce
Business Consultant and Psychologist

iUniverse, Inc.
New York Lincoln Shanghai

USING LEAD MANAGEMENT ON PURPOSE
CREATING EXCELLENT PRODUCTS AND SERVICES FOR A GLOBAL ECONOMY

iUniverse books may be ordered through booksellers or by contacting:

iUniverse
2021 Pine Lake Road, Suite 100
Lincoln, NE 68512
www.iuniverse.com
1-800-Authors (1-800-288-4677)

Because of the dynamic nature of the Internet, any Web addresses or links contained in this book may have changed since publication and may no longer be valid.

The views expressed in this work are solely those of the author and do not necessarily reflect the views of the publisher, and the publisher hereby disclaims any responsibility for them.

ISBN: 978-0-595-44832-6 (pbk)
ISBN: 978-0-595-69249-1 (cloth)
ISBN: 978-0-595-89151-1 (ebk)

Printed in the United States of America

To my three children:
Michele, Stephanie, and Leanna.

Contents

Part I   Choice Theory®—Lead Management's Core

Part II   Managing for Quality

Part III   Putting It All Together

List of Illustrations

As far as we can discern,
the sole purpose of human existence is to kindle a light
in the darkness of mere being.

—Carl Gustav Jung, 1875–1961

Acknowledgments

While one or a few people may write a book, it takes many to create it. Like other authors, I have a list of people to whom I owe a debt of gratitude for inspiring me to take on the joy and pain of writing.

The first is Bill Glasser, who read my mind and heart, and asked me to rework his original publication *The Control Theory Manager*. While I only had a dream of writing someday, he assumed I could do it. Next would be John Demartini, who through his work has offered me the opportunity to discover my purpose and understand how writing was its next manifestation.

I am especially grateful to my family: Anna, my wife, who is a constant and stable source of support and challenge to everything I do; my three wonder-filled daughters, Michele, Stephanie, and Leanna, who keep me grounded with their affection and humor; and Hunter, my first grandchild, who doesn't care about what I do—he just loves me.

Special thanks goes to Linda Harshman, executive director of the William Glasser Institute, for her thoughtful, insightful, and continuous assistance. In addition, Christina Gaudet warrants a special mention for her creative illustrations. In addition, the inspired comment of Brian Landry referenced in Chapter One; the catalytic call of Charles Hicks and the encouragement of an old friend, Paul Hickey need notice. Finally, a special thank you goes to my daughter Stephanie who took the time to draw some illustrations and to review an early manuscript.

Foreword

I remember I was in eastern Canada speaking at the official opening of the newest school to achieve the Quality School designation: the Beaverbrook School in Moncton, New Brunswick. Scheduled to speak in Charlottetown, Prince Edward Island, the next day to a group of educators and members of the business community, I traveled with Ken Pierce. As we drove over to Prince Edward Island, we discussed the applications of Lead Management principles to business and organizational development. Ken had been outlining some of the challenges facing some of the various companies in eastern Canada with which he had been working over the last few years.

Ken asked me if I had considered updating *The Control Theory Manager*, a book I had written in 1994 to reflect the recent developments of my ideas for application in the business community. I wrote *The Control Theory Manager* to focus on utilizing Choice Theory® principles in leadership and management to ensure the production of quality products and services at a time when the U.S. economy was struggling with its foreign competitors. Updating this was something that had been on my "to do list" for some time, and, when Ken raised it, I thought here was just the person to do it. Now we have a well-established global economy, so the principles and practices inherent in Choice Theory® and Lead Management are even more relevant today.

Ken, a registered psychologist and experienced corporate trainer, is a long-standing Senior Faculty Member of the William Glasser Institute and has extensive experience in utilizing Lead Management in business applications. As well, my own work focus had been away from business and on our educational system. Moreover, it was moving quickly back into the mental health field. Therefore, I asked Ken if he was interested in rewriting *The Control Theory Manager*. He said he would need to think about it, and, after we discussed it further, to my delight, he readily agreed.

What you hold in your hands is the result: a new, revitalized and updated work—*Using Lead Management on Purpose!* I am confident you will be as pleased as I am with *Using Lead Management on Purpose!* I read *Using Lead Management on Purpose!* in one day, and I really enjoyed it. It's a great book! It is clear and concise on principles and practices. I am very enthusiastic about the uses for

Ken's book. In addition, it is so much better than before—much clearer. I learned a lot of Choice Theory® when I read it. It will offer you lots of ideas and tools to take to your organization. The realistic examples that he presents drew me, also. As well, the key points highlighted and the chapter summaries made it easy for me to get at the crux of the material. Finally, my perceptions of Snow White's potential as a Lead Manager shifted.

Using Lead Management on Purpose! will give you the latest ideas and techniques for applying Choice Theory® principles to business. It is chock full of ideas, tools, and examples so that you can apply Choice Theory® and Lead Management to any business, whether private or public sector and whether to produce a product or a service. I invite you to *Use Lead Management on Purpose!* and see how it will assist you in your work.

William Glasser, MD
Los Angeles, April 2007

Preface

Modern economics dictates that we all adjust to a global economy. The success of our efforts in making a global economy work hinges on our ability to work together in effective relationships that are purposeful for all concerned. Dr. William Glasser's Choice Theory® model is still the cutting edge of much of our most successful approaches to building and sustaining successful relationships. His own institute operates in some sixteen countries around the world, a testament to the value and effectiveness of his approach.

His original 1994 publication of *The Control Theory Manager* addressed the application of Choice Theory® to leadership and management, which is termed Lead Management. This work addresses the scarcity of attention in business literature to expanding the ideas, techniques, and applications of Lead Management to the economic times in which we now live.

In my own experience over the last twenty years as a business consultant and corporate trainer in the private and public sectors, I have noticed this recurring void. With so many diverse factors at play, specific issues get lots of attention but there is little focus on the foundational underpinnings of what makes it possible to compete in a global economy.

When I had the opportunity to speak with Dr. Glasser about this he shared my concern. Therefore, when he suggested that I rework his earlier book, it was an opportunity to do something close to my heart. *Using Lead Management on Purpose!* is the result of that endeavor. In *Using Lead Management on Purpose!*, the reader will find the ideas and tools needed to get at the crux of what makes it possible to provide excellent products and services at a competitive cost in a global economy.

Introduction

The purpose of every business or organization is to create a high quality product or service at a cost its market will bear. The purpose of the owner, manager, or supervisor is to ensure that this occurs regularly by managing the workers hired to produce the high quality product or service.

This was the primary premise that Dr. William Glasser started with when he first wrote *The Control Theory Manager* over fifteen years ago. Since then he has evolved his ideas and terminology, and that evolution is reflected in many of his later works—most notably *Choice Theory®: A New Psychology of Personal Freedom* in 1998. On a drive from Moncton, New Brunswick to Charlottetown, Prince Edward Island about three years ago, I queried Dr. Glasser on whether he had considered writing an updated edition of *The Control Theory Manager* to expand on his work in applying Lead Management to the business community. He said that he had considered it but that his current commitments precluded it. Then he challenged me to do it with his assistance. This is the result of that conversation. So, let's pick up that same thread and continue.

The common understanding of a managing or supervisor relationship is that one person, the boss, tells the workers what he wants done with little or no input from them. The manager also sets the standard for what he wants done and evaluates the workers on how well they are doing it. If they are not doing as well as he wants, the manager motivates them with threats of discharge, or a loss of pay or promotion. Less common motivators are the offer of more pay or more interesting work.

However, the traditional "carrot and stick" or "reward and punishment" approach ignores that humans are the only animal that thinks about thinking. In other words, they can disassociate or stand outside themselves and consider other useful perspectives. Because this is so, humans are not externally motivated but rather internally motivated by what they value about themselves and their world. Like all objects in the universe, every worker has a purpose and when they see how their work connects to their needs, values, and purpose, they will readily offer their energy, creativity, and commitment to the production of a high quality product or service. A satisfying relationship between the manager and those being managed which honors the values of both the worker and the manager is the most powerful driver to productivity.

It is not that carrot and stick does not ever motivate. If the work takes little or no training and there is a large pool of workers desperate for a job, those with jobs will work harder or make an effort to look like they are working harder. Nevertheless, even in hard times, workers who do not believe the manager cares about them as human beings, with needs and values of their own will resist authority by absenteeism, low quality work, and pilfering from the workplace. There are countless ways that employees who do not believe they are valued can hold onto a job and still do little more than the minimum.

There is little in traditional, coercive Boss Management that can lead to a satisfying relationship between the manager and the workers. The manager can get the hands of the worker but their brains and hearts will focus elsewhere. Instead, they are more likely to use their creativity and energy to get away with doing as little as they can. The rare worker will apply his creativity to enhance the work if he does not feel valued.

While this book will focus on managing paid workers, almost all parents use boss managing in their attempt to rear successful, cooperative children. Warm, caring teachers also start to boss when their boss threatens them to get the test scores up on mandated tests. Coaches stop teaching and begin to boss as they struggle to turn out winning teams. Even directors and producers will boss temperamental artists in an effort to turn out award-winning productions. In these instances, where money may not be the dominant factor, the limitation of the reward and punishment approach to manager-worker relationships is that it distracts from purposeful productivity.

Despite threats and punishment, children defy their parents, students have no interest in their subjects, athletes pay little attention to their coaches, and performers become difficult and temperamental. Eventually some coercive parents, teachers, coaches, and directors begin to sense that bossing does not work very well, but most of them are at a loss for what to do differently or afraid of losing control of the situation or both. This book specifically addresses how managers can replace bossing with leading. When they do, they discover that a warm, respectful, and shared-values relationship between leaders and those they lead are the most effective human relationships.

There is an additional management problem that typically occurs in situations where the power between the managers and the managed either is close to equal or is thought to be close to equal by the person being managed. Typical examples of this situation are business partners, husbands and wives, parents with grown children, and middle-aged children struggling with stubborn, elderly parents.

In these situations, one or both of the parties may try to boss the other based on the firm belief that he or she knows what is right for the other party better than the other party does. However, the people in the examples above, most commonly marital partners fight back against bossing by the other. In these situations, where money may be a factor but rarely a dominant factor, they refuse to meet expectations and reject the authority of their partner. Not recognizing and respecting each other's values in these situations is often a disaster. The relationship goes off balance and improving it becomes an imperative.

Using Lead Management on Purpose! provides the reader with both the concepts and tools to address these situations and relationships. Let us begin.

PART I

Choice Theory®
—Lead Management's Core

Let us begin by exploring the underpinning of Lead Management, which is Choice Theory®. In order to understand why Lead Management works and what Choice Theory® is all about the next four chapters will be devoted to this important task. In coming to understand Choice Theory®, you also find out how powerful the Lead Management approach is in moving from mediocre to quality products and services. Our journey begins with a brief story.

Snow White: A Boss Manager
(With apologies to Jacob and Wilhelm Grimm)

Once upon a time, in a far away kingdom, there lived a beautiful princess named Snow White. Like many people of royal blood down through the ages, naïve and unaware described her approach to life. Having grown up the daughter of a king, watching her father rule his realm, she felt she had learned many useful things about leadership. With this knowledge under her tiara, Snow White left the security of her parent's kingdom to seek her fortune in the big, wide world. She traveled for many days and searched in many places for an opportunity to make her mark on the world.

One day she came across an enterprise that she thought was ideal for her. It was a small diamond mine with only seven employees. These workers happened to be dwarfs. One of them, called Doc, oversaw its operation. While the mine was running smoothly, there was some dissatisfaction among the six staff, especially from Grumpy, Sneezy, and Dopey, concerning Doc's leadership.

Snow White concluded that these men were ill suited to the demands of a modern business in a competitive marketplace. They seemed to lack consistent dedication to the task and were prone to bouts of singing and dancing, both on and off the job. While these men also worked hard and seemed to enjoy their labors, Snow White felt they lacked both the sound leadership and good management practices to be successful. She decided that they could produce not only more diamonds but also better diamonds if only they worked smarter and with more motivation. Having watched her father run a kingdom, she felt confident she could tell them how to run a small mining operation to improve its bottom line both quickly and efficiently. All seven dwarfs were impressed with Snow White's credentials and sophistication. They also liked her promises of bigger profits. Therefore, they all agreed—Doc somewhat reluctantly—to let her manage their operation and follow her orders so that they could improve the quality and quantity of their production.

Snow White began immediately to reorganize the entire operation, designing specific tasks for each employee and then closely supervising them to ensure they each did their assigned tasks correctly. She also scrutinized the production line constantly and pointed out every flaw she could find and told them how to correct it. She held a weekly staff meeting in which she reviewed their work and instructed them in how to improve it. Snow White did not waste time collecting their perspectives with long discussions of how the work could be done, but rather trusted what she knew had worked for her father in his successful rule. She was sure that she was right in her assessment of the needs of these employees and this organization. All they had to do was worker harder and smarter by following her instructions and things would improve.

As you can probably guess, the staff went along with her direction and leadership for a while, trusting that she knew what she was doing. However, when the quality and quantity of their production actually began to decline instead of rising, they began to wonder. Her response to this was that they were not working hard enough or were not listening carefully enough to her directions. Moreover, when they really pressed her, she blamed them for spending too much time singing "Hi Ho, Hi Ho ..."

What the seven dwarfs did not realize, and more importantly, what Snow White did not realize, was that she suffered from three illusions, or limiting beliefs that would ensure the demise of the mining company, she was leading. Snow White's first illusion was that she knew more about mining than her employees. Her second illusion was that she did not need their input to create a quality product. Her third was that she could make people produce a quality product if only she gave them enough resources and direction.

Snow White had learned a traditional approach to leadership and management that came from a different time. She tried to prepare the dwarfs for business world that no longer existed. However, Snow White did the business community a great service by highlighting some of the primary reasons why many organizations fail to remain competitive today. Fortunately, for the seven dwarfs, Snow White left her management position rather quickly, before things could get much worse. Her departure was the result of her naivety about the apple industry.

♦   ♦   ♦

This book explains exactly what it is going to take to enable modern business to provide a quality product or service at a competitive price. You will come to understand where Snow White went off track and what you can do in your organization to avoid going off track in the same way, thereby ensuring it remains viable.

Chapter One

Leading through Relationships

Education makes a people easy to lead, but difficult to drive; easy to govern, but impossible to enslave.

—Lord Brougham

The "Aha!" occurred when my friend Brian said something that stopped me cold in my tracks,

> You know Ken, my supervisor can buy my time and my attendance at work, but if he wants my creativity, enthusiasm and commitment, I have to choose to give it to him.

Brian's simple and profound statement captures the essence of and reason for this book. Many managers, based often on their own life experiences, are convinced, like Snow White was, that they know *why* the people they manage behave the way they do and *how* to get them to work hard. It never occurs to them that they could be wrong.

Perhaps they have forgotten a similar experience that often occurs in growing up and in parenting. One day, every mother and father realizes that, regardless of their child's age, they cannot really make their child do anything the child does not want to do. If you have ever tried to make a child eat something she did not want, whether three months or thirteen years, you have probably experienced this. Everyone has the capacity to refuse to cooperate and will ultimately only do what they choose to do. Moreover, they will only choose to cooperate when it serves what they value the most.

Brian's comment as an employee and the experience of most parents both fly in the face of what many managers and adults call "common sense." Moreover, many managers have missed the vital lesson that is the very essence of this book.

This lack of awareness of what really motivates people is why so many managers (and parents) are puzzled. Managing workers by ignoring what they value is not leading to the quality work needed to be competitive. For example, in the private sector where old style management continues, domestic automakers continue to lose market share by offering a lower quality product to higher quality foreign imports. Moreover, this occurs even though domestic manufacturers offer low or no interest loans while foreign manufacturers do not. In the public sector, the situation is very similar. The public, so disenchanted with the poor service from public agencies, supports a growing trend to privatize traditional public services to both improve the service and cut the costs. A recent example in both the United States and Canada is health care.

That many companies and organizations are failing to achieve quality is painfully apparent. In the private sector, former customers are buying what they believe are better foreign products. These products are better mainly because foreign workers have leaders who manage them more effectively. In the public sector, citizens are seeking traditional community services, such as health care, from private sector sources in the hope of a better quality service.

Due to the work of Edward Deming in the late 1940s, many companies have broken with experience and so-called common sense to embrace a management system, Lead Management that consistently produces quality. Many other companies continue to use Boss Management, a traditional system that has always produced a lot of work and was quite competitive as long as everyone else used it and no one's product was significantly better than anyone else's. In the next three chapters, I offer you detailed descriptions of both systems so you can see for yourself, which is best. This is necessary because managers need more than a description, they need a clear understanding of why Lead Management produces quality and Boss Management does not and cannot do so.

To produce a quality product or service requires not just careful thinking, but also, a high level of awareness of the different levels of thinking, usually not known to traditional boss managers. Lead Managers, on the other hand, are usually consciously aware of the need to operate at several thinking levels to get the job done.

Consider the diagram (Figure 1.1) below, adapted from the work of Robert Dilts, which describes the Hierarch of Being, or five levels of thinking used by Lead Managers in the workplace.[1] One can think at a behavioral, strategic, belief, identity, or spirit level. Each lower level is included in the one above it. For example, our spirit, or connection to the universe, establishes our identity, which is how we see ourselves in the world, from which our values emerge, which reflect our belief system. These beliefs determine our strategies of thinking and coping, which determine our behaviors. These behaviors present themselves in the workplace. We all use these levels of thinking to define ourselves in the world. However, the Lead Manager adds this awareness to his role in the workplace.

Figure 1.1 The Hierarchy of Being

Lead Managers have an acute awareness of, and an ability to operate at, all levels of thinking while a traditional boss manager usually has awareness and ability to operate in only the bottom two levels, strategies and behaviors. This ability to operate at and move between all five levels is what makes Lead Managers inspiring individuals, able to convince workers to produce a quality product or service. It is this awareness of the workers' needs to be able to connect their work to their entire being that makes the difference in producing a quality product or service. This is the insight that Lead Management brings to the business community. When you marshal people's energy, creativity, and commitment, only then will they bring their special genius to your workplace. Then they will be operating at all levels of the Hierarchy of Being because they will be able to think at all levels.

Consider workers and imagine describing the five levels of their being, i.e., the ways they interact with the world. This Hierarchy of Being is particular to a person's situation. It is located in an environment—the plant, office, institution, community—where the worker performs his or her job. At the bottom are the behaviors the workers choose to use in this environment such as acting energetic or acting passive, acting creative or acting bored, acting loyal or acting disloyal. Above that are the strategies—the ways of thinking required to carry out the behaviors. For example, a worker who wants to behave energetically may tell himself, "I will do the best job possible!" A worker who is acting bored may have as her strategy, "I will only do enough to get by." Above the strategies are the beliefs that determine the strategies. An example of a belief is feeling like a valued part of a team or organization or feeling like just another cog in a big machine. Above the beliefs of the worker is the identity of the worker. The identity is the source for the beliefs below it; such as "My job is an important part of who I am!" or "My job pays the bills!" At the top is the spirit, which is the how the workers see their jobs as purposefully and consciously connected to their world such as, "My job is part of how I manifest my own destiny," or "My job here is not really about me or my dreams."

Edward Deming's post war work with the Japanese recognized that the higher up in the hierarchy you address your communication to the worker, the greater the impact on the person, the workplace, and the organization's bottom line. This is how the Japanese were able to rebuild their society and economy so quickly after World War II. The rebuilding connected closely to the spirit, identity, and beliefs of the Japanese people. This is also, what Choice Theory® recognizes and Lead Management addresses so effectively. When an inspired Lead Manager links the organization's product or services to the workers' spirit, identity, and beliefs, she ignites the workers' energy, creativity, and commitment (strategies and behaviors) to produce quality in the workplace.

Choice Theory® is a new explanation of how we behave and provides the tools needed to communicate at all levels of the workers being. In this book, I will suggest that all managers learn to use Choice Theory® if they desire quality products and services for the competitive marketplace. Workers managed by people who use Choice Theory® will consistently do quality work at a competitive cost.

It is only fair to alert readers that Choice Theory® is challenging to use because doing so requires us to give up the external or extrinsic, reward and punishment psychology that most of us have learned and used all our lives. We cling to this ancient psychology, even though many of its flaws are obvious because, until the recent introduction of Choice Theory®, there was nothing to replace it. Choice Theory®, in a form that is understandable and usable, has only been around since the early 1980s. Still, its acceptance is growing rapidly, and my experience in teaching this theory is that people who read it with an open mind find it to be so sensible and usable that many of them give up traditional bossing and begin leading.

To achieve quality, Lead Managers, using the concepts of Choice Theory®, embrace the following two procedures, which rarely ever occur to boss-managers:

a. Learn what quality is, share it with everyone in the organization, and listen respectfully and carefully to any worker with an idea on how to improve it.

b. Manage everyone in the organization so that it is obvious that it is to his or her benefit to settle for nothing less than quality work.

This book focuses on managing people. Moreover, it is the inspired leadership approach of Lead Management, which offers the direction to higher quality products and services. This book does not deal with non-human issues such as statistics, flow charts, finances or technology. While these procedures are essential to managing a successful organization, companies are not failing because they lack this technical expertise; they are failing because they are trying to control people rather than trying to lead them. While you can control resources like money, equipment, and facilities, you cannot control people—you can only lead them.

Many people seem unwilling to learn that workers will not do high quality work, not because they do not understand the technical aspects of the job, but more because of the way boss-managers treat them. They seem to ignore the obvious: that providing quality products or services require that every worker offer as gifts to the company or organization his or her energy, creativity, and commitment. This can best happen in a Lead Managed environment and is much less likely in a traditional one of Boss Management.

This book addresses all managers in both the private and public sectors. In the private sector, managers need to learn to lead workers so that what they produce sells for a reasonable profit. The amount of profit, however, will also depend on the company's ability to convince customers to buy. The surest way to do this is to produce quality products and to render quality service. Advertising is important, but no matter how convincing it may be, if it promises more quality than the product delivers, disappointed customers will stop buying and may never buy again. It is the quality at a fair price, far more than advertising, which determines long-term profitability.

In the public sector, the challenge is very similar. As public sector organizations come under increased public scrutiny and move towards a stronger business focus, there is increasing demand on every public sector manager to justify not just expenditures but also the very existence of the organization. With outsourcing now a common practice, public sector managers are even finding themselves in competition with the private sector for services that they have historically provided. Yet the public sector manager who continues to use Boss Management cannot provide quality services or products to her organization's clientele. Only public service workers who are willing to give their energy, creativity, and commitment to the workplace can provide quality services. This requires the use of Choice Theory® based Lead Management approach.

Many people at the top of unsuccessful companies believe that fear is an important motivator. Choice Theory® explains why it is not, and why workers who are not fearful produce quality work. In addition, the theory shows that the more respectful, need satisfying the treatment of the workers, the more energetically, creatively, and loyally they apply themselves, thereby increasing the quality of their work. More than most management consultants, Deming talked about joy in work. Joyful workers perceive themselves as valued so they bring their energy, creativity, and commitment to the workplace—the essential foundation for quality products and services.

Any organization that strives to provide quality products and services is like a triangle, as in Figure 1.2. To achieve quality there is a need for a vision upon which rests the resources of the organization, which has developed processes to create quality. However, the foundation for the entire structure—that which holds it all together as a stable, productive, and profitable organization—is the relationships between the people who work there.

Figure 1.2 The Foundation of an Organization

The production of quality products or services demands relationships based on the seven values cited in Figure1.2: leadership, trust, respect caring, fairness, teamwork, and loyalty. These are the same values, which most people strive to base their family lives. Therefore, it is not surprising that workers who produce quality often say they feel like they belong to a family when they are at work.

What the Japanese did, when they moved to Lead Managing without knowing the underlying theory, was unusual. It may have been that their desperate effort to get their economy going after the destruction of World War II opened their minds to new ideas, but more likely it was because their culture places high value on roles and relationships. The Japanese, like other eastern cultures such as the Chinese and the Koreans, holds great respect for the need to appeal to all five levels of the workers' being. So, their organizations are more like large families that feel dependent on each member to contribute their very best to achieve the goals of the organization. As a result, they think long term and hire employees for life, and they continually challenge workers to give their energy, creativity, and commitment to the organization. In addition, they are much more willing to listen respectfully to people who they believe are experts. China's current and rapid rise to economic importance is in part due to this ability to listen carefully to experts from all over the world and to work together.

During my employment in a postsecondary institution, I had the opportunity to travel to China and see first-hand their keen interest in listening to and learning from experts. My role, along with a colleague, was to train twenty instructors from technical colleges across China in competency based education [CBE] principles and practices. Competency based education is a training approach which emphasizes leader directed student based learning rather than the traditional, authoritarian teacher based teaching. It relies on learning specific knowledge and skills directly related to an occupational area. It has been shown to be very effective is accelerating occupational training in a number of countries around the world. China's plan was to transform over three thousand technical schools to a competency based education model within ten years. CBE was one of the tools they had decided to adopt to speed up their economic growth. This process continues today with an active, ongoing exchange of students and faculty from China.

Unlike their Chinese counterparts, American and Canadian business leaders, even when their companies are losing money or making much less than before, still tend to see themselves as successful managers. When their businesses fail to perform up to expectations, they blame unfair competition, poorly educated workers, the high cost of capital, excessive government regulations, overblown legal expenses, or union demand much more so than they blame their own inability to lead workers. They are confident that their success relates to their experience and common sense and have little faith in anyone who does not believe as they do. Their lack of awareness of the other levels of a worker's being indicates that we often pay lip service to new ideas much more than we pay attention to them, especially if they suggest the abandonment of established practices that we often refer to as common sense.

To translate Lead Management into practical experience, I am going to introduce you to three imaginary organizations: a private sector manufacturing firm called Jerri Inc. a public sector service agency—The Millennium Community Hospital, and a small business enterprise called Dave's Gas & Grocery.

Jerri, Inc.

Frank is the CEO of Jerri Inc. a medium-sized manufacturing plant with over 300 workers that supplies specialized components to the electronics industry around the globe. Frank learned about the manufacturing industry from his own father who ran a small plant in their hometown, and he has been in business for over ten years. His business grew quickly in the early years when the electronics field was developing rapidly.

Frank takes great pride in his efficiency and that of his people and his plant. In fact, he has often remarked that he is only on this earth to create manufacturing processes that are more efficient. Frank is driven by a personal purpose of always making things more efficient wherever he can.

Frank has two vice presidents, Anne and Gene, who report directly to him and who supervise ten team leaders each. The team leaders head up groups of fifteen workers who are on the line producing, packaging or shipping the specialized components.

The Millennium Community Hospital

Marie is the director of The Millennium Community Hospital, a large public institution in an industrial city. Her hospital provides a wide range of health services to the entire city. She has more than three hundred staff members at her institution including physicians, psychologists, social workers, nurses, public health nurses, licensed practical nurses, nutritionists, home care providers, and administrative and support staff.

Marie is a single women very focused on her career. She continually looks for ways to enhance her knowledge and skills in her job. She enjoys learning new things and actively seeks out opportunities to do so. She has an MBA and extensive experience in managing a variety of public sector organizations. Marie's often-stated mission or purpose is to provide the most up-to-date level of service to the hospital's clientele.

Marie has two assistant directors, Raymond and Jacqueline, reporting to her. Both Raymond and Jacqueline each supervise several teams of ten to fifteen specialized professionals. Each team offers a range of services to a sector of the city.

Dave's Gas & Grocery

Dave is the owner and operator of Dave's Gas & Grocery, a twelve-pump gas station and convenience store that is open twenty-four hours a day, seven days a week. He has two teams of staff headed up by Joe and Rose who work rotating twelve-hour shifts. He has an excellent location near the city's main exit.

He has been in this operation for over four years and is starting to believe his is a viable business. This is Dave's third entrepreneurial venture, and, this time, he feels he has found his niche. A car accident three years ago widowed him, and he thinks that he can build a stable future for himself and his twin daughters by anticipating the needs of his customers.

Dave is eager, focused and devoted to his business success as much as he is to his young family. He puts in long hours himself and expects his staff to do likewise. Dave always asks himself how he can anticipate his customers' next need.

All three organizations are committed to providing the best quality product or service to their respective clientele. The staff of these three organizations will be appearing throughout the book to demonstrate important aspects of Choice Theory® and Lead Management. You will see them behaving as both Lead Managers and boss managers so that you will be able to notice right away the significant differences between the two approaches to leading others. We will be calling on these teams to demonstrate how Choice Theory® and Lead Management move organizations forward.

The next chapter will help you discover how understanding values is one of the secrets to why Lead Management make the best managers.

Seven Key Chapter Points

1. The foundation of an organization is the relationships among the people who work there.

2. People actually operate at five levels of being: spirit, identity, beliefs, strategy, and behavior.

3. People's values internally motivate them in both their personal and work life.

4. You cannot make anyone do something he or she does not choose to do.

5. High-caliber, quality products and services can only arise from high-caliber, quality relationships.

6. People only contribute their energy, creativity, and commitment to other people whom they perceive as valuing them.

7. The most effective workplace relationship is one of warmth, respect, and trust between leaders and the people who work there.

Chapter Two

Value-Driven Behaviors Create Relationships

And when we think we lead, we are most led.

—Lord Byron

Anne noted to Gene after a strategic planning meeting at Jerri Inc.

Anne has captured an important aspect of the workplace. So often workers feel restricted and scrutinized by the behaviors of their managers, and this gets in the way of quality. Since all we do is behave in some way we often forget that we choose almost all our behavior. For example, when we manage an unproductive worker, we choose what we do and the worker we manage chooses what they do. Therefore, our ability to succeed in managing depends on how well we learn to choose behaviors that are more effective.

Bosses choose Boss Management, but it is not an effective behavior because few bossed workers will choose to make quality products or perform quality services. In competitive industries, managers who are not willing to learn to lead will preside over the destruction of their companies. Many companies realize the importance of quality and strive to achieve it, but most have not succeeded because their boss-managers are unwilling to give up bossing. This is because, following their common sense, they believe in a psychology that tells them that bossing is correct.

To review briefly, boss-managers, like almost all human beings, believe in and manage according to the traditional theory of human behavior: external control psychology. They follow it mostly because it supports their common sense belief that people can be made, through reward and punishment, to do what the manager wants them to do, whether they like it or not. To some extent, boss-managers follow the theory because no one has ever offered them another. They have nothing to turn to if they suspect, as I believe many do, that what they believe may be ineffective. Therefore, it is not that they believe in external control psychology so absolutely that they cannot change. Rather, for almost all people, external control psychology reflects their current level of awareness.

Choice Theory®, applied to human behavior, is quite new. Although its description appeared as early as 1973, it first appeared in a form that people could use both in their work and in their life in Dr. William Glasser's 1984 book, *Control Theory*. It is so new that even Deming, who taught about how to manage people, did not teach it. Deming's practice preceded Glasser's Choice Theory® that supports it, actually a very common situation. For example, before Magellan circumnavigated the globe, actually proving it was round, sailors sailed as if the world was round. In a similar way, those who accept Choice Theory® will do so because it makes more sense than external control psychology and, when applied to management, it works. Workers managed by Lead Managers who follow Choice Theory® do quality work, whether they realize they are following it or not.

However, once managers learn and begin to use Choice Theory®, there is a good chance that they will give up bossing and choose to become Lead Managers. They make this choice because they have learned that people function at five levels of being and with this knowledge, they are able to make constant improvement in the way they manage. It is the same with sailors. Those who knew the world as round navigated much better than those who sailed as if it was round but did not actually know it.

Many companies installed unsuccessful programs intended to enhance quality. Often these programs came from a by top-down edict and comprised of a duplicate of some program that was successful in some other company. However, imposed, copied programs usually negate the energy, creativity and commitment that create quality. Unless you understand the theory behind it, trying to copy someone else can lead to chaos. As Ralph Waldo Emerson noted, "envy is ignorance; [and] imitation is suicide."[2]

Until taught differently, most managers will continue to believe that they can make people do what they do not want to do. This illusion—Choice Theory® claims we cannot make people do what they do not want to do and external control psychology claims we can—is the fundamental difference between the two theories. As practiced by almost all people, stimulus response theory assumes that a stimulus triggers human behavior, which is an event or a situation that is outside the behaving person.

Therefore, if we do not choose to answer a ringing phone or do not choose to do quality work that a manager is trying to persuade all workers to do, it is because, at this time, neither answering the phone nor doing the quality work is satisfying enough to one or more of the five basic needs. We do not always follow the expectations placed on us. If the expectations do not sufficiently match up with one or more of our basic needs, we will not choose to meet it.

Choice Theory® has basic needs, and stimulus response theory has stimuli. Stimuli are just information. By itself, information does not make us do anything. It tells us what is going on, but it is still up to us to figure out how to do that which is best for us. Choice Theory® explains that what is best for us is always what we believe is most satisfying to one or more of five genetic needs built into our brain. Our value system reflects these needs.

This leads us to the basic difference between boss-managers and Lead Managers. The boss-manager thinks that he can stimulate the worker into doing what he wants, usually through threats or punishment, regardless of whether this is satisfying to the worker's needs. The Lead Manager knows that all he can do is give workers information. Based on that information, it will be up to the worker to decide if they should do the quality work needed for the company or organization to succeed. To help workers decide that producing quality work meets one of the five basic needs, Lead Managers give workers information that will persuade them that expending the effort to do quality work will satisfy them and honor their values better than anything else they could do at that time. Humans have genetic hard wiring so that workers subconsciously know about the five basic needs, but Lead Managers must to be conscious of these needs so they can assist their workers in fulfilling them. Managers cannot give a worker need or value-satisfying information unless they know what the needs are.

The Five Basic Human Needs

Guiding the creation of a human life, from conception on through the rest of that human's life are the 30,000 genes present in the zygote. Genes are the instructions for what each individual is to become physically; they are responsible for the color of our eyes, the shape of our nose, and all else that will make up our physical structure and the physiology. Scientists believe that it takes considerably less than the 30,000 genes to do this structural task, which leaves the function of many genes not yet identified.

What Choice Theory® postulates is that some of these excess genes have nothing to do with our structure or physiology, but instead govern human behavior. All humans exhibit certain common behaviors to some extent such as a resistance to danger and an affinity towards things that look like human babies. So all of us live our lives in certain recognizable ways, and we do this because our brains, driven by these behavioral genes, are constantly telling us what to try to do. Choice Theory® has broken these myriad needs into five generalized categories of needs, referring to them as the five basic needs.

These needs are: (1) survival; (2) freedom or choice; (3) power or recognition; (4) love and belonging; and (5) fun or progress. Our hand is a good metaphor to represent and remember our five basic needs. (See Figure 5.1.) The thumb of our hand could represent our survival need, the pointing finger our need for freedom or choice, the index finger our need for power or recognition; our wedding ring finger our need for love and belonging and finally, the little finger, our need for fun or progress. Our history of successes and failure in getting these needs met evolve into a value or belief system. This value system represents what [people, events, objects, etc] we believe is most efficient or effective in getting these needs met.

Figure 2.1 Five Basic Needs

A more detailed explanation of each of the basic needs follows.

The First Basic Need: Survival

We can feel the push of survival whenever we are afraid, hungry, thirsty, cold, or tired. It is the primary human need, and all the other basic needs have probably evolved from it. We also feel the drive for survival sexually in that we struggle for sex so that the species will survive. We realize that in humans there are other genetic motivations for sex such as love, power, and fun so, because it is driven by at least four of the five needs, the human sex drive is strong and long lasting.

The Second Basic Need: Freedom

We live in a reasonably free society and political leaders extol the virtues of freedom every chance they get. Freedom is really about having choices about the things that are important to us. However, talking about freedom and choices and practicing it are two very different things. The attitude of "he who pays the piper calls the tune" dominates many workplaces.

In the beginning, freedom was a requisite for successful survival, but it soon became a separate need. No one reading this book would seriously deny that. When workers struggle in boss-managed workplaces, freedom is on their minds much of the time. Lead Management is more democratic. To the extent that we can manage people in a way that they have some freedom of expression and a manager who listens and honors their values, quality will increase. Dominated workers will spend too much energy struggling to gain a sense of freedom, which is taken from the pursuit of quality work.

The Third Basic Need: Power

The need for power becomes most obvious in boss-managed workplaces where coercion, a misuse of power, is the modus operandi. Unfortunately, as bosses coerce, quality suffers. For most of us who do not have or want the opportunity to boss, the need for power is satisfied not through coercion, but through the belief that people will listen to us and act on what we have to say. Lead Management could not work if Lead Managers did not get satisfaction from the idea of persuading workers instead of coercing them. Respected workers asked for their input, given useful work, and encouraged to evaluate what they do—the conditions for quality—will have their power need met in Lead Managed workplaces.

The Fourth Basic Need: Love

All humans need to feel loved. Friendship, or a sense of belonging with others, is a vital part of this need. The need for love probably evolved out of the need for survival. The human species cannot survive if its infants do not survive, and its infants do not survive without an immense investment of time, energy, and resources. Love evolved as a strong, separate need to ensure that the adults make this investment. Many parents are willing to make remarkable sacrifices to save the life of a child. The more a manager can foster a sense of friendship and belonging in the workplace, the higher the quality of work. Workers who do not believe that anyone cares about them personally tend to work only for survival, and this is hardly a motivation for quality work.

The Fifth Basic Need: Fun

Considering fun as just relaxing and enjoying ourselves is actually superficial. Within Choice Theory®, fun means that we need to feel that we are learning and progressing in important ways that reflect our value system. When we laugh, usually considered fun, we are actually gaining a new or fresh perspective on something. Between travel and entertainment, perhaps the most money goes to the search for fun than any of the other needs. Fun is a basic need because it is the genetic reward for learning and evolving ourselves. We travel to learn and feel like we are growing as individuals. We are born knowing less than all other higher animals about how to survive. Moreover, we have the most to learn in order to survive and satisfy our needs. Evolution has provided fun as an incentive to learn and progress as a species.

◆   ◆   ◆

Although there is differences in what will satisfy each person, most people want similar amounts of freedom, power, love, fun, and the means to survive. They are similar, at least, in the sense that all human traits, both physical and psychological, follow a normal statistical distribution. For example, there are no adults taller than nine feet or shorter than one foot; the vast majority of us are between five and six feet tall. Although a few people will give up and die when things get hard, most of us will struggle very hard to survive. Still it would be foolhardy not to be aware that there are differences in the strengths of the needs that workers bring to their job. For example, it might be unwise to hire a person who has a stronger than normal need for love and belonging for the lonely, isolated job of night watchperson.

Of the five needs, four are psychological. Only the need for survival is physiological in that we think of survival as the need for food, water, sex, shelter, and safety. In this book, we will concentrate on the psychological needs—freedom, power, love, fun—as it is the satisfaction of these needs in the workplace, far more than the need to survive, which leads a worker to do quality work. This does not mean that workers do not think of their job as a means to survive. However, few workers will do quality work based on satisfying this need alone. If survival is all they believe the job provides, they will rarely do more than is required to keep their job.

If we want quality, we have to structure the work so that it will satisfy much more than survival. For example, people managing workers who have relatively secure jobs, such as in the public sector, must offer strong psychological benefits if they want workers to do quality work. Job security alone, as is often in the case with government work, assures many government workers of their survival, but does not meet any of the other, psychological, needs. Accordingly, government workers often produce poor quality work. Later, in Chapter Seven, I will address managing public sector workers so that they get their needs met and produce quality work.

◆   ◆   ◆

No one can satisfy another person's needs. We all must do this for ourselves. What we, as Lead Managers, can offer is the opportunity. It is up to the worker to agree that what the manager provides is, indeed, a need-satisfying opportunity, and to take advantage of it. For example, we can get our workers together, explain to them what we want done, and ask them to come up with ways to achieve it. When they make suggestions, we can listen to them, help them explore the ideas, and encourage them to evaluate what they are now doing. Most workers find their needs for love or belonging and power satisfied with this approach. These needs seem to be the hardest to satisfy at work, but with Choice Theory®, it is simple.

This approach is satisfying to workers because, this way, they believe that they have more control over what they are doing and thereby have a clearer opportunity to meet all their basic needs at work. Control is another basic component of Choice Theory® and part of our freedom need. We all want to have a sense of control over what we choose to do. Only when we feel in control in our lives and work are we able to honor our own values. While we have no choice but to try to satisfy our needs, and since we have to behave to do this, the more we believe we are in effective control of our own behavior, the better we are able to carry out the instructions of our genes and honor our own needs or values. This compelling drive to meet our needs within our value system Demartini cites this way, "The only reasonable expectation you can have of people is that they will live according to their own values."[3]

The better we satisfy our basic needs, the more in control we feel. This feeling of control helps produce quality.

So, in Choice Theory®, quality is anything we do or learn that is highly satisfying to one or more of our basic needs. When people try to force us to do things we do not want to do, because we do not find it need satisfying because it does not honor what we value, we feel as if we have lost control of ourselves. What we may also feel is that our lives are losing quality and any connection to our values. Similarly, when forced by lack of money to buy a low quality product or suffer poor quality service, we feel as if we are losing control. On the other side of the coin, if we have plenty of money but a quality product or service is not available, it is likely that we will feel the same lack of control. This causes pain. According to Choice Theory©, all pain is the result of a loss of control, which prevents us from satisfying our basic needs.

So, having a sense of control in satisfying our needs within our values—psychological as well as physiological—is the motivation and intent of our lives. We can no more deny the importance of our psychological needs than we can deny that to survive we must breathe. Gaining freedom, power, love, and fun is not as urgent as breathing, but these needs are vital. We feel compelled to live out our values; it will hurt too much to do otherwise.

Suicide—a tragic but, unfortunately, too common behavioral choice—usually is contemplated or carried out when a person has lost a lot of freedom, power, and love. A person may also kill himself when he is faced with starvation or freezing, but that is extremely unusual. We make a mistake when we fail to appreciate the strength of the psychological needs and their relationship to one's values and needs.

How long a person can endure need-frustration will vary from person to person, depending on the strength of the need and the capacity to satisfy it. However, if the frustration goes on too long, a person feels the pain of this frustration just as acutely as when she feels pleasure when she is in effective control of her life. What is important, here, is to understand that we cannot escape from the pain of being unable to satisfy our genetic assignments. The planets move around the sun in a specific, predetermined pattern, so too our needs make up a fixed, genetic part of our biology.

Not knowing or not accepting Choice Theory®, boss-managers act as if the people they manage somehow suspend their needs and values or subordinate them to the need of the boss when they are at work. This is not true. The only thing that is predictable about a human being is that they will always live inside their own values and strive to satisfy their needs. At their best, bosses are pleased if the people they manage enjoy themselves at work, but most do not manage as if this is important to them. At their worst, they manage in a way that workers find it difficult, if not impossible, to satisfy their needs to the extent that they would like. Since most bossed workers believe that they need their jobs to survive, they are willing to put up with frustration. They do not like it, though, and they will rarely do more than they have to do to keep their job. Lead Managers know that doing quality work never crosses the mind of a frustrated worker expected to ignore his own values.

Not only do frustrated workers not produce quality work, they often actively try to do the opposite, becoming adversaries to the boss. It is difficult to be in contact with an adversary and not act on that frustration. At work, this is the most destructive of all situations. Overtly or covertly, depending on how much power the worker perceives the boss to have, the worker fights the boss. To fight someone when there is little hope of winning wastes a lot of energy. People say that working on a frustrating job is draining, and this statement is exactly right. Bossing drains energy from what is available to do the job well. Bosses worry that if they give power to the workers they, themselves, will lose power. The exact opposite is true. Workers are so appreciative of getting some power, some control, that they respect the person who gives it to them.

◆   ◆   ◆

Let us look at four points that describe a boss manager. (See Figure 2.2.)

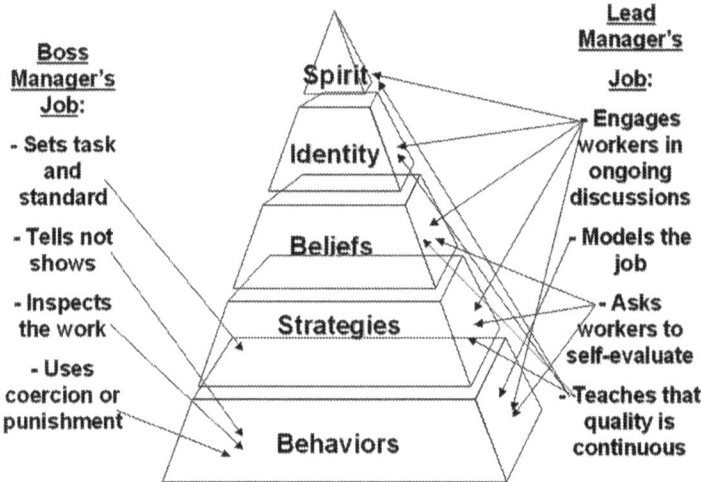

[1] The boss sets the task and the standards for what the workers are to do. Bosses do not compromise on the task or standards. Instead, the worker has to adjust to the job as the boss defines it or suffer the consequences determined by the boss.

[2] The boss usually tells rather than shows the workers how the work is done and rarely asks for their input as to how it might possibly be done better.

[3] The boss, or someone she designates, inspects the work.

[4] When workers resist, as they usually do in a variety of ways, all of which compromise quality, the boss uses coercion—usually punishment—to end

the resistance. In so doing, the boss creates a workplace in which the workers and managers are adversaries. Bosses think that this adversarial situation is the way it should be.

As you see, none of these points is concerned with giving any freedom, power, friendship (love/belonging), or fun to the worker. Together these points send a clear message from the boss: if you do not do what I say, I will punish you in whatever way I can. However, to succeed in persuading the workers to do the quality work that we need today, leaders are required. Benevolent dictators are not enough.

Now look at the four elements of Lead Management, and see how much more the leader is concerned with the workers' needs and values—especially their need for power. (See Figure 2.2.)

[1] Lead Managers engage the workers in an ongoing honest discussion of both the cost and the quality of the work needed for the company to be successful. They not only listen, but also encourage their workers to give them any input that will improve quality and lower costs.

[2] The Lead Manager, or her designate shows or models the job so that the worker who is to do the job can see exactly what the manager expects. The Lead Manager works to increase the worker's sense of control over the work they do.

[3] The Lead Manager eliminates most inspectors and inspections. He or she teaches the workers to inspect and evaluate their own work for quality with the understanding that they know a great deal, almost always more than anyone else, about what high quality work is and how to produce it economically.

[4] The Lead Manager continually teaches the workers that the essence of quality is constant improvement. To help them, he makes it clear that he believes his main job is as a facilitator. This means he is doing all he can to provide them with the best tools and workplace as well as a friendly, non-coercive, non-adversarial atmosphere in which to do the job.

Now that you have a thorough understanding of the needs, I will explain the next element of Choice Theory®: behavior. To lead successfully, a Lead Manager must be aware of the fact that behavior is more complicated than most of us realize. The next chapter addresses this.

Seven Key Chapter Points

1. You cannot impose Lead Management on others, but you can teach and model it so others are encouraged to explore it.

2. You cannot reward or punish a worker into doing quality work, but you can give the worker information and support, and challenge him to achieve it.

3. The physiological survival needs and the psychological needs of freedom, power, love and fun motivate workers.

4. A worker's psychological needs for power and love or belonging are a major part of why he or she works.

5. Lead Management creates an environment where a worker can meet all his needs and honor his personal values.

6. Lead Management provides an opportunity for the worker to achieve a sense of control and therefore freedom and power over her work.

7. Lead Management creates a need-satisfying workplace where the worker feels part of an adventure that enables him to contribute his energy, creativity, and commitment.

Chapter Three

Every Behavior Is a Value-Driven Total Behavior

Economics is the science, which studies human behavior as a relationship between ends and scarce means, which have alternative uses.

—Lord Lionel Robbins

At Dave's Gas & Grocery, Rose and Joe were talking at the pumps when Rose said,

> Yesterday I was so frustrated. The diesel pumps weren't working properly and Dave chewed me out as if I had done something wrong. Doesn't he realize I was doing my best?

This remark highlights a recurring issue in the workplace: self-control is an integral part of managing others and a common cause of poor quality.

As explained in the last chapter, the cause of all behavior is our constant attempt to choose what we believe will best satisfy our needs and honor our values. Therefore, if a worker does quality work, she chooses to do it because it is more satisfying than if she did not make this choice. Assuming she knows how to do quality work but does not, this, too, is a choice. This choice is motivated by what she is asked to do, and how she it is asked. If the work or the request to do it is not satisfying enough to her personal needs and values to persuade her to make the effort, then she is unlikely to do so.

In addition, a Lead Manager will not use this knowledge of Choice Theory® to accuse a worker of choosing to do less than he is capable of doing because doing this will only make a situation worse. The accused worker will usually get defensive and deny the accusation vehemently because self-respect is a high value for most people. He will rarely admit that he chose to do something shoddy or thoughtless.

Workers will say, "I didn't realize I was doing this," or "I don't know how it happened that I did that," or "I couldn't help it," or "What else could I have done?" as if better behavior were impossible. It is not, and the manager's main task is to persuade workers to choose to do the quality work that they are almost all capable of doing. However, it will take skillful managing to persuade some workers to make these quality choices. The best way for managers to gain these skills is to learn how Choice Theory® explains behavior. The explanation is more complicated than most people realize.

The Webster's New World Dictionary definition of behavior is: (1) the way a person acts and (2) responses to stimulation. The first definition is incomplete; the second, as explained in Chapter Two, is incorrect. While every behavior includes some activity, Choice Theory® is unique in explaining that behavior encompasses much more than activity. It is a combination of four components; activity is only one of those components. The other three are thinking, feeling, and physiology.

Let us explore this for a minute. Consider the behavior of jogging. The physical activity of running and moving the head, arms, and legs is one component. What we think about as we run is another ("I am going to run a mile today."). How we feel, (excited and energized) as we run, is a third. In addition, what our heart, lungs, and muscles do (increased respiration, pulse, muscle tension) is the fourth, physiological, component. The four wheels of a car with front wheel drive, as seen in Figures 3.1 and 3.2 can represent each of the four parts metaphorically. We control the car by turning the steering wheel, which directs the front wheels, which connect to the motor powering our car. Then the back two wheels will always follow in the direction of the front wheels. The same principle applies with the behavior of jogging with the action of running, and thinking about running, and thinking about ourselves running, generating a specific feeling and a specific physiology within our body.

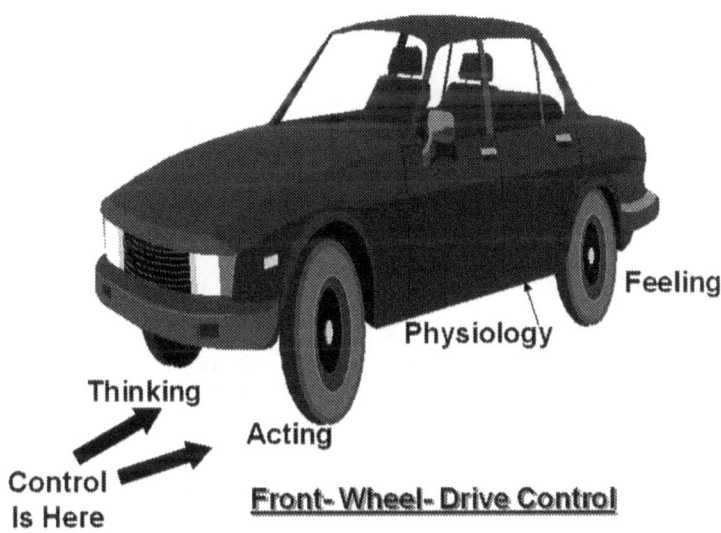

Figure 3.1 A Total Behavior

In Choice Theory®, every behavior is a total behavior—total because it is always the sum of the four separate components: actions, thoughts, feelings, and physiology. While we will discuss these components separately, they are actually never separate in the same way that the car's four wheels are never separate. Each component is always present as part of the whole or total behavior.

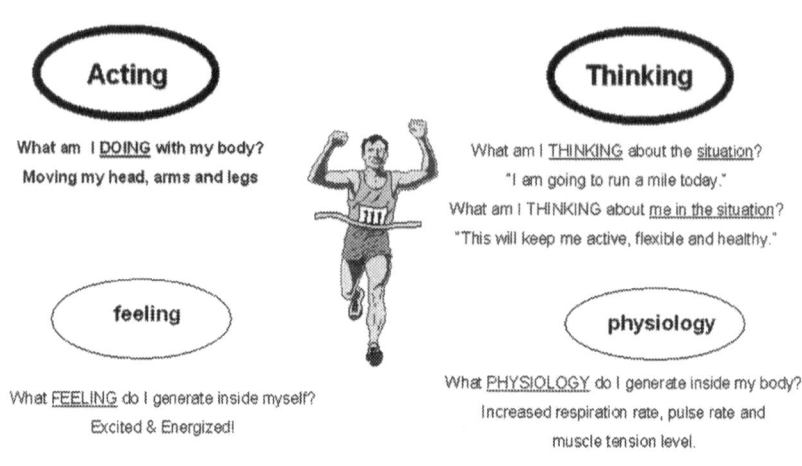

Figure 3.2 A Total Behavior of Jogging

As long as we are conscious, or at the steering wheel of our behavior car, the two front wheels of the four, acting and thinking, are voluntary and under our control. The other two rear wheels, feelings and physiology, are rarely directly under our control. However, we gain control indirectly by using the front wheels. Let us look at another example: golf. (See Figure 3.3.)

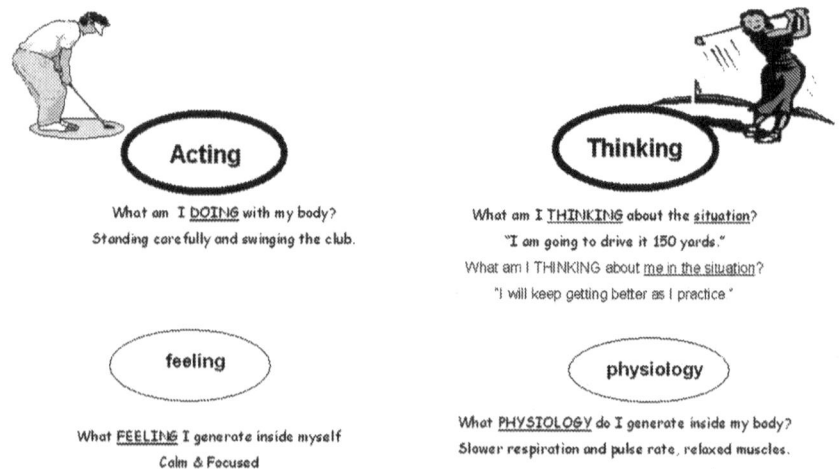

Figure 3.3 A Total Behavior of Golfing

Pretend you are on a golf green right now, setting up a shot. Notice how you are thinking about the shot you are making, then notice what feeling you are generating inside yourself. Finally notice what physiology you generate inside your body. The combination of these four components you would call golfing. The complete behavior of golfing requires you to take control of the steering wheel of your behavior car and direct the front two wheels (actions and thinking) to create the feeling and physiology in the back wheels. If you decide to do and think something else, you will create a different feeling and physiology in your body. If you decide to sit down on the grass and think about your current debt load, you would probably generate very different feelings and physiology. What's more, you would not be golfing. Change one of the components, and you change the complete behavior.

As another example, we regularly choose the total behavior of eating. First, we experience hunger pangs. We then think about eating and sit down to eat. We choose this total behavior knowing we will feel better and be physiologically healthier. If we decide to lose weight, painful as a weight-loss diet may be, it is often a choice based on our desire to be healthier and more attractive. We do not choose the pain, but we know from experience we cannot avoid it.

◆   ◆   ◆

Of the four components, how we feel is probably the most important to us. This is because our feelings tell us if the behavior we are choosing is effective or ineffective. If it is highly satisfying to one or more of our needs and values, we feel satisfied and believe we have chosen a more effective behaviour. If it is frustrating, we feel unsatisfied and immediately realize that what we have chosen is not effective. For example, we choose total behavior "A" over "B" or "C" because we believe that, in the predictable future, "A" will feel more satisfying than "B" or "C." Therefore, in choosing what we do, we are always trying to continue or increase what feels satisfying or to discontinue or reduce what feels unsatisfying—to seek pleasure and avoid pain.

As important as our feelings are, often we pay little attention to them. As long as we do not feel strongly, we tend to be more aware of our actions and thoughts. For example, if you are deep in thought while playing golf, you might even skip lunch. You are so engrossed that you are not even aware of feeling hungry. However, when we feel very good or very bad, we pay a great deal more attention to how we feel. In these extreme situations, we often become much more aware of our feelings than of the other three components.

From the Lead Manager's standpoint, if an employee feels bad, the manager's main responsibility is to help him better satisfy his need, and that usually means to act and think more effectively on the job. For example, you could team him with a skilled, friendly worker; suggest he improve his skills by taking training the company offers; ask him to take charge of a small project so that he experiences more recognition; or, if it seems needed, encourage him to tell you what may be on his mind.

Regardless of what it is the employee needs to do to feel more satisfied, when he succeeds, what he has done is change from one total behavior to a better one. In doing so, he has changed how he acts and thinks. Therefore, it is on actions and thoughts, the front wheels of the behavior car that a Lead Manager focuses. He accepts feelings and physiology and understands how important they are, but he concentrates on what the worker has control of—his actions and thinking—and can change because he knows that this is the only way to alter the worker's feelings. Think of it this way: the whole is the sum of its parts, and if you change a part, specifically the actions or thinking, you change the whole.

It is important to understand that it is possible to choose to feel bad. Most of the time, we are unaware that we are actually making this choice. The painful choice comes from our belief that, if we did not make it, we would feel even worse or we might choose to do something that worsens the problem. For example, as miserable as it is, most of us are capable of choosing to feel depressed when we mess up on an important assignment at work. We are not aware of this choice, but it comes from the idea that our manager will treat us better if we are suffering. He may even excuse our poor work or offer to get us some help. If we did not choose the depression, there is the possibility that we might choose to get angry and unfairly attack others, which would make the whole situation worse.

Very early in life we learn to make these miserable choices when we mess up. For example, we learn to choose to cry and be distraught when we spill our milk. When it happens, we may actually think the spill is funny, but we know that if we laughed our parents would get upset. We choose to cry instead. As we grow, we become less and less aware of our choices because if we continued to be aware that we are even capable of choosing pain and misery, we would feel stupid and ashamed—feelings which are both highly frustrating to our need for power. By the time we are adults, we may be very unaware that these are choices. However, if a manager is aware of what is going on, he can help employees make more need-satisfying, value-based choices.

Among the most common forms of misery, we learn to choose, although we are usually unaware that they are choices, are depression, anxiety, common illnesses such as colds and stomach upsets, some allergic conditions such as hives, and some physical pains such as headaches and backaches. However, these choices are complicated in that once we choose one or more of these miseries, there is nothing we can do directly to stop the pain or illness because we are not aware that we are making a choice. A doctor may give us a drug such as Valium that, in altering our physiology, may make us feel better for a while, but drugs are not a solution to the problem because they do not deal with the basic need frustration that was the cause of the miserable choice in the first place.

Aware or not, people who make these painful choices fail to understand that they are actually choosing a total behavior that is made up of more than the feeling and unhealthy physiology. It also includes acting and thinking, and these we can change. If you are managing a person who whose work has deteriorated, and you suspect he is choosing to be depressed to avoid responsibility for the poor quality of his work, you will know that he cannot help himself. He is no more aware that he has a choice to act and think more effectively than he is aware that he is choosing his misery.

Your job is to talk to him supportively, to listen to him, and to persuade him that he can actually do something better on the job if he chooses to make the effort. In the beginning, you look for an area in which he has competence, and with your support, can experience success. Tell him you will check on his progress to see if he needs more help, but you do not want to hear why he cannot do it; you believe he can. If he does, he will gain confidence, continue to improve, and, with these new acting and thinking choices, stop experiencing the pain and misery of depression. Later, you might give him this book, so he can learn what he did that worked.

When we choose more need-satisfying actions and thoughts, we give up the old self-destructive choices that fail to satisfy our needs. From the standpoint of management, the self-destructive choices cost huge sums of money and reduce the quality of its product or service. As bad as the loss of money is, the reduction in quality in a competitive market is far worse. The abuse of legal and illegal drugs is a common coping strategy in the workplace. It is rare to employ many people without having a few who abuse alcohol. They are risking their jobs in a desperate effort to feel better. Using "alcoholic thinking," they often go so far as to bring a bottle to work and sneak drinks on the job. To implement this decision, they must act and think, but, due to the alcohol, they are unaware that their ability to act and think effectively is actually seriously impaired.

If you were a boss-manager and you caught an employee drinking on the job, you might threaten to fire him unless he stopped. You would have told him to stop doing what he was choosing to do, but you would not have helped him to make a better choice. Still frustrated, he would likely get angry and rationalize that you, not his choice to drink, are the problem. Confronted with threats from a boss-manager and unable to figure out how to change, he may even drink more heavily, file a complaint, or report sick and spend a lot of company money on medical care that will not address the real problem.

A Lead Manager may also tell an employee who is an alcoholic that his job is at risk, but she will then go on and help him make a better choice—a choice not to drink. As long as an alcoholic keeps on drinking, it is unlikely he will choose a better total behavior and he may think he is doomed to be a drunk. Lead Managers who have learned Choice Theory® know that we cannot just stop doing anything without changing to a more effective behavior. To do this, we often need help. As the Lead Manager of this employee, you must be willing to counsel him at least to the extent of persuading him to seek professional help. Suppose he chooses to attend Alcoholics' Anonymous (AA) regularly, stops drinking, and, once again, is an effective employee. What he has done is much more than just stopped drinking. He has changed his total behavior, and he is now thinking and acting much more effectively because he is no longer experiencing the physiologic impairment brought on by his choosing to drink. Now healthy, he tells you he has not felt this good in years. As alcoholism is a pressing problem in many companies, I will explain more about how to deal with alcoholic employees in Part 3 of this book.

Seven Key Chapter Points

1. Every behavior is actually four distinct parts: an action, thinking, a feeling, and a physiological response.

2. How we act and think generates our feelings and physiological responses.

3. Workers behave in certain ways, not only to meet their needs but to equally honor their values.

4. A worker's feelings are the best measure of whether he is meeting his needs.

5. Self-control comes from taking control of what we do and think, thereby giving us control of our feelings and our body's internal state.

6. Self-control is a necessary ingredient to building quality relationships, which create quality products and services.

7. Everyone has the capacity to choose more need-fulfilling behaviors if they can connect such behaviors to their needs and values.

Chapter Four

We Want Our Value-Based, Quality World

One always dies unsure of one's own value and that of one's work.

—Gustave Flaubert

At the local Chamber of Commerce meeting, Marie commented to Frank,

You know Frank, I like to think I contribute a lot to the hospital, but I am not sure how well I do it since I only supervise my own team and get very little feedback.

Marie has identified a common concern of managers: how to measure quality. This chapter will consider how we develop our personal criteria of quality.

Since we must satisfy our needs in the real world, we have to be equipped with a way to find out what that real world really is. This leads us to what, at first glance, seems to be a silly question: How do we know that there even is such a thing as a real world? William James, the father of American psychology, recognized that this was an important question. To get his students thinking about it in the 1890s, he would query them with questions like, if a baby were born with no senses (meaning no vision, hearing, touch, taste, or smell) and was kept alive what would be inside his mind when he reached eighteen years of age?

What James was driving at was the fact that the only way we can find out there is such a thing as the real world is that we are born with the capacity to sense it. Having no senses, whatever was in that eighteen-year-old's head would be restricted to what he was able to imagine; he would have no inkling of what actually existed. Helen Keller proved we do not have to have all our senses to find out there is a real world all around us, but we have to have some of them. Therefore, our senses are the vehicles by which we measure the quality in our life.

By themselves, our senses, do not tell us that the world exists. They are just outposts of a complicated perceptual system that exists in our brain, and it is through the working of this whole system that we actually discover the world. How this occurs is too complicated for this non-technical book. Suffice it to know, that, even though the system is complicated, humans easily use it. By the time we are a few years old, we are already capable of recognizing most of what goes on around us enough so that we can name things. Very early in life, we become especially capable of recognizing and naming people that feel good to us such as mother and ice cream. So early on, we become interested in what feels good, or bad, and we build a collection of such experiences.

Imagine for a moment you are holding a bag of collected marbles, half are yellow and the other half are red. Each marble represents a significant life experience you have judged as either good (yellow) or bad (red). This bag of marbles is like your memory bank of important life experiences. We will tend to believe what we need to believe to make sense of all of these marble experiences together. This bag of marbles, or belief or value system, will not necessarily be logical or consistent or even reflect the laws of science and nature. Yet we will persist in believing in these values for three specific reasons. First, they enable us to make sense of our own personal life history. Second, they help us feel safe in the present. Third, they enable us to prepare for our future needs. Because these forces are so strong, this value system is stable and takes a significant new learning to alter it. We adjust or replace a value only if we have sufficient information to warrant such a transformation.

In the learning process, we take in a lot of information. In order to manage it we unconsciously engage in three activities. One of the things we do is delete or ignore information that does not feel good or bad and is therefore not important to us at that point in time. Another thing we do is distort information so that it reflects, to some degree, our experiences. The final thing we do is to generalize information to enable us to use it effectively in other situations in the future. We use these three processes to create greater efficiency and the result is a sort of condensed version of our experiences that becomes our value system. Our value system reduces into about seven personal core values, which reflect our critical experiences and summarize our bag of marbles efficiently.

Both our yellow and red marbles serve us in unique ways. Moreover, we store bits and pieces of our yellow and red marbles in a special place in our memory that Glasser calls our *quality world*. It is like a personal photograph album or a collage of parts of experiences or imaginings that we have had which we set aside. In it we store what we have discovered feels good and balancing to us at one or more levels of our Hierarchy of Being. Much of it is stored as pictures of people, places, and things, and as word pictures of need-satisfying ideas or values. Often this quality world will also contain associated sounds, tastes, smells, and textures that go with the images. We do not know—unless we learn Choice Theory®—that this knowledge connects to highly need-satisfying experiences. What we do know is that these people, places, things, and ideas feel balancing and satisfying to us.

The specific knowledge that makes up our quality world becomes the core of our lives, the core of our Hierarchy of Being. (See Figure 4.1.) We unconsciously add to it as we live, but we do not add anything that does not feel satisfying and balancing to our Spirit, Identity, and Beliefs. We also replace things from this world when they no longer fit, and once we do, we lose interest in them.

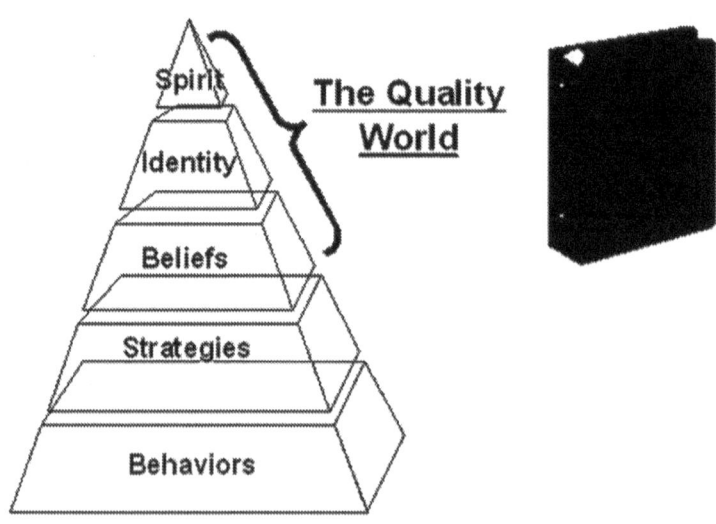

Figure 4.1 The Quality World

Using Choice Theory® language, all of us are functioning as control systems. We are continually trying to control or manipulate the real world so that it is as close as we can make it to our quality world. Even though we are trying to satisfy our needs, it is not needs that actually drive our behavior. Rather, it is the specific, highly need satisfying values that we store in our relatively small quality world that is the driving force of our lives.

For example, a child does not want love she wants a loving mother. It is through the loving mother that she gets the love. We almost never search for abstractions such as love or power. Our quest is always for very specific, concrete manifestations, such as mother, when we try to satisfy our need for love.

In the same way, Dave, the owner of Dave's Gas & Grocery, probably gets a lot of his need for love and belonging met, not just by his own family relationships, but also by his relationships with his two teams of workers. In addition, one of the ways Marie gets her need for power and recognition met is by chairing a hospital committee planning the Christmas party. In addition, Frank at Jerri, Inc. gets both his power and love needs met partly through his relationships with some of his larger corporate clients.

The quality world in our mind allows us to define the concept of quality: quality is whatever we choose to store in our quality world. For each of us, that, and nothing else, is quality. This means that each of us has total control over what we put into our quality world. This also means that there can never be an absolute definition of quality. However, since we are of the same species and many of us live in similar cultures, much of what is in our quality worlds is similar. For example, a product such as Coca-Cola™ is successful because the company has created something that many people have decided to put into their quality worlds.

When we say that our quality world is the most important part of our lives, we mean, for example, that we do not listen attentively to people who are not in this world and we do not want a product that is not in it or that we are not considering putting in it. We will not believe an idea or accept a value that is not in our quality world. If it is in this world, it is quality to us even if destructive. For example, alcohol is a part of the quality worlds of all alcoholics.

If we are to manage successfully, if we are to be Lead Managers, we must convince people we manage to put what we ask them to do into their quality worlds. In order to do this, the people we manage have to put us into their quality world first. Lead Management is the most effective way to manage people so they both put the manager and/or the product or service into their quality worlds. Lead Managers succeed in gaining access to the quality world of the people they manage because they are sensitive to the worker's needs. Therefore, when Frank at Jerri, Inc. made some time in his busy day to sit down with Gene to discuss Gene's plans about returning to school part time and showed a willingness to modify Gene's shift hours to assist him, he was encouraging Gene to put him into his quality world. Gene will put Frank in his quality world only if he perceives Frank's offer of assistance to be genuine. Bosses who coerce, threaten, and do not seem to care about the needs of the workers are the last people workers will put into their quality worlds. This is the short, accurate, Choice Theory® explanation of why bosses have so much trouble getting workers to do quality work.

It is possible that a worker will do quality work because he finds the work itself satisfying, regardless of how he is treated. But, as work gets broken down into more and more pieces, and fewer and fewer workers have access to the finished product, it is more how the worker is managed than the work itself that determines whether the worker will do the quality work necessary for a company to be competitive.

To maintain a competitive edge every company needs to base all decisions on how well each decision both persuades and then maintains (1) the company, (2) the managers, (3) the product and services, and (4) the customers in the workers' quality world. If most of the workers put all four of these factors into their quality worlds and the company keeps improving the product and keeps it cost competitive, then that company will prosper.

The domestic automobile industry is a classic example. This is an industry whose managers have not persuaded enough workers to put the company, the managers, the product, and the customers into their quality worlds. This has led to a decline in the quality of many domestic cars. Moreover, this decline has led many previously good customers to remove these cars from their quality worlds. Keeping its products and services in the quality world of its customers is the true bottom line of every company.

Once customers decide to take a company's product or service out of their quality worlds, there is little that most companies can do to persuade them to change their minds. Domestic auto companies have lost their places in too many of their former customers' quality worlds to non-domestic competition. It is proving difficult and expensive to get back what they once had so completely.

We will not usually take something out of our quality worlds unless there is something to replace it. Many customers are loyal to an American or Canadian product because "Made in the USA" or "Made in Canada" is a strong part of their quality worlds. If we depend on advertisers to sell the product through celebrities, an appeal to patriotism, a low price, or a picture of a bunch of young, happy people using the product, they may succeed for a while. However, a long-term satisfied customer is by far the best advertising there is available.

It is the same for managers. They must show a real concern for the workers' needs. Slogans, prizes, or sales contests will not keep a poor product or service profitable. To do this, managers have to learn to do something that many managers have not considered doing: put the workers they manage into their quality worlds. If they refuse to do this, it is unlikely they will be able to become Lead Managers. Lead Management is a two way street: both workers and managers must put each other into their quality worlds. Managers who are unwilling to walk both up and down this street will not be capable of managing for quality.

The needs, total behavior, and quality world make up the heart of Choice Theory®. If you understand this much, you are well on your way to knowing what is needed to become a Lead Manager. There are still a few concepts that I will cover in Chapter 5, but if you understand this much, you will have no trouble learning what remains.

Seven Key Chapter Points

1. All people believe what they need to believe to make sense of their personal histories.

2. A value system is a summary of core beliefs gleaned from personal history.

3. For efficiency, we delete, distort, and generalize our perceptions of the world to create and maintain our value systems.

4. We store bits and pieces of what we find most need satisfying in our value systems in imaginary photo albums. These albums make up our quality worlds.

5. The content of each person's quality world reflects three specific levels of the Hierarchy of Being: Beliefs, Identity and Spirit.

6. We all function as control systems continually trying to make the real world as close as we can make it to our quality worlds.

7. Quality for an individual is whatever he or she chooses to store in his or her quality world, so the Lead Manager's task is to get himself, the work and the customer into the worker's quality world.

Chapter Five

Building Balance Frees Energy, Creativity, and Commitment

A vital element in living dreams is the ability to remain centered and balanced, no matter what happens.

—John F. Demartini

At Jerri Inc. Gene heard a member of his team comment to her coworker,

This observation speaks volumes as to how managers miss the genius of workers that is essential to producing a quality product or service. Let us look at this now.

In the previous chapter, I explained that the knowledge that is stored in our quality worlds is the picture of what we are trying to accomplish with our behavior. For example, previously I said that we do not answer a phone because it rings. All the ring provides us with is the information there is someone on the other end of the line who wants to talk to someone on our end. We answer only if there is a picture of answering a phone and talking to whoever is on the other end as a need-satisfying activity in our quality world. If we do not have that picture, we would never actually answer a ringing phone.

The actual reason we answer when the phone is that there is a large difference between what we want (a value)—to talk to someone on the other end—and what we have (a void)—just the phone ringing. It is this difference, the void between what we want, which is stored in our quality world, and what is now happening in the real world, which is the specific cause of all our behavior. Our perceived voids drive us toward our values.

For a worker to do quality work, a manager who is in the worker's quality world must ask him to look carefully at what he is doing and evaluate it in terms of what he believes is quality. If this evaluation tells the worker that the work he is doing is not quality, the manager must then ask him to compare it with what he knows is quality, which is in his quality world. When he makes this comparison, he will immediately see that there are specific differences (his void) between the qualities he wants (his value) and what he is now producing. He will then be motivated to work harder and move from good enough work to quality work.

He needs to keep evaluating what he is doing and to keep improving it. In so doing, he puts the idea of constant improvement into his quality world. This is only logical since he will be continually adding to his quality world with new knowledge, skills, and experiences. In this way, the product or service upgrades continuously over time.

Once a worker puts the pictures of quality work and continuous improvement into his quality world, he will have no choice but to work hard, especially if he has a picture of the manager and customer in that world. As he does, he will work to produce a better and better product or service. The result is constant improvement, but to ensure that this occurs managers must give their workers some important additional supports.

If they are to put a picture of continually improving quality work into their quality world, workers need managers to give them tangible gestures of appreciation for doing this. Specifically, they want managers to trust them to evaluate their own work. The workers know that they have this trust when the managers accept that they are producing quality. What I am describing here is the evolution from bossing to leading, from checking all the workers do to trusting them to do the very best they can. Once this trust is established, quality is also established. The respected business leader Warren Bennis noted, "... the trust factor will reign as the most pivotal factor of a leader's success ..."[4] From that point, the only concern of the workers and managers is to agree on a fair way to compensate the workers for their contribution.

Constant improvement requires more than hard work on the part of the worker. It also requires that the worker be creative and add this creativity to his output. This creativity is a manifestation of all four top levels of his Hierarchy of Being. (See Figure 5.1.) To assure that he will contribute this creativity, this special genius, the Lead Manager must be willing to listen to him if he wants to do something new. Boss-managers do not often think about creativity, especially if it arises from the worker. In the minds of boss-managers, workers are supposed to do what the boss says with no exceptions. Boss-managers tend to think concretely about the work and, to them; creativity is something mysterious that is only available to a few special people.

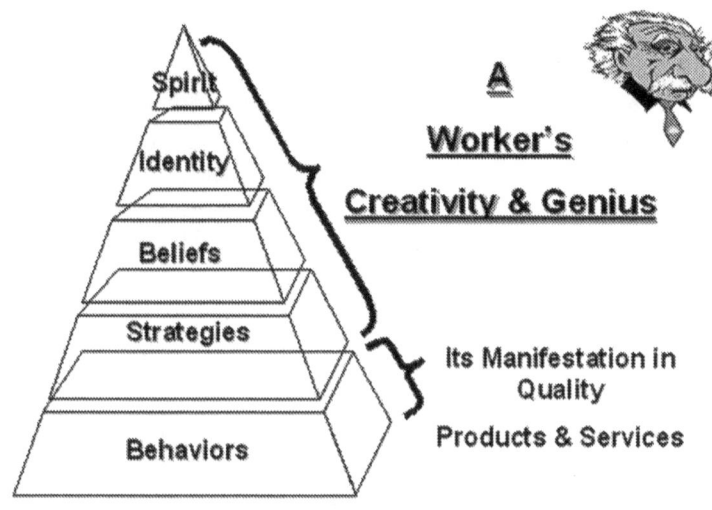

Figure 5.1 A Worker's Genius

It is nonsensical to some to imply that every worker is a sort of genius, but in fact, there is increasing evidence to suggest that. Recently, Carol Abraham, health writer for Toronto's *Globe and Mail* and author of *Possessing Genius: The Bizarre Odyssey of Einstein's Brain* made this very point. Her book is the story of Dr. Thomas Harvey, the pathologist who retained Albert Einstein's brain after his death. Dr. Harvey spent almost forty years distributing slices of it to various medical research establishments around the world looking for anyone who could say how Einstein's brain was unique. She reports that Albert Einstein's brain is just like yours and mine, no significant differences at all.[5] So, logically, then each worker has the same species-specific brain as Einstein and so the same capacity for genius in what they do. Lead Managers operate under a similar assumption about their people, and one manifestation of the worker's genius is the creativity they display at their work.

In *Organizing Genius The Secrets of Creative Collaboration*, Bennis and Biederman express it this way, "Successful groups reflect the leader's profound, not necessarily conscious, understanding of what brilliant people want. Most of all, they want a worthy challenge, a task that allows them to explore the whole continent of their talent."[6]

Choice Theory® teaches that we are all creative and that this creativity becomes most available to us when we feel we are in control. Under these safe and relaxed circumstances, we all tend to be creative, but the catch is that there is no guarantee that our creativity will be usable on the job. We tend to become increasingly aware of both our creativity and how we might use it to improve what we do when Lead Management is succeeding. In other words when there is only a small difference between the quality we are accomplishing and the quality we want, Lead Management is flourishing and excellence is guaranteed.,

If we become aware of a creative idea or procedure, we will not try to put it in practice unless we are confident that the idea and we will receive respect. Therefore, a Lead Manager is supportive in that she makes a point of telling her workers that they should feel free to tell her about any good ideas they have. She will listen. However, an inspired Lead Manager goes even further. She observes her satisfied workers and looks for creativity. When she sees it, even in an embryonic form, she talks with the worker, asks him to explain what he is doing, and encourages him to go further with it.

Therefore, a Lead Manager who understands Choice Theory® will also understand creativity. He will know that each worker brings a valuable and unique set of experience and skills to work. He will know that their special perspectives on their own jobs are available and could create more quality for the organization. Since no one can predict where or when valuable, usable new ideas will make an appearance, the Lead Manager's job is to ensure a nurturing environment is present to tap this priceless resource. Everything he does will encourage workers to pay attention to their creativity and share it with him and others who might be interested. He will tell the workers that they should not be hasty in judging the usefulness of a new idea.

For example, Frank of Jerri Inc. might say to Anne, about an idea she has for streamlining a production line, "Think about it and do not hesitate to share it with me even if on the surface it seems to have little usefulness. It could have a spark that together we could kindle to the benefit of all."

This impresses workers. They spread the word that the manager is interested in new ideas, and this turns loose the kind of creativity that leads to gains in quality. These gains are not possible without this tangible support. If we are not capable, as boss-managers usually are not, of tapping the creativity of those we manage, we will not come close to discovering the new and better ways to do a job or solve a problem that are the core of quality.

Bosses put a damper on creativity. They know the job and there is only one way to do it: their way. Their workers tend to work for a paycheck, and their pay mainly makes up the difference between what they want and what they have. Bossed workers tend to pay no attention to their creativity because they know it is not wanted; no one will listen to them anyway. Stifling creativity, which is easily stifled—a derisive look may do it—may be the worst effect of Boss Management. They make it impossible to reach the level of quality that is available to Lead Managers who are aware that how they treat workers will either tap or turn off their creativity.

However, even worse happens when workers are bossed and stifled. Since how they want to be treated is so different from how they are treated, they use their creativity to bolster their efforts in the war between workers and bosses. When an adversarial relationship exists between these two, not only is energy lost but, when workers are fearful for their job, this creativity can appear as sickness or physical pains in the fearful workers. Frustrated workers getting psychologically creative on the job unconsciously create many pains and illnesses.

Companies led by managers whose workers have them in their quality worlds have much lower medical expenses, absenteeism, accidents, and work disruptions than companies whose workers are bossed. Bossing leads to dissatisfaction, which causes expensive waste and misery. The failure of many of our major industries to produce competitive products is the price we pay for bossing workers. For those managers willing to learn Choice Theory®, it is a price they can avoid paying.

Seven Key Chapter Points

1. Lead Managers understand that being in their worker's quality world enables the worker to be self-motivated towards quality.

2. Through self-evaluation, the worker, because of trust in his job expertise, strives to reduce the gap between what he sees in the real world and what he wants in his quality world for his product or service.

3. To tap their creativity workers will need to feel listened to, respected, and acknowledged for their contributions to continuous improvement.

4. Every worker brings to his job a special genius that can only be uncovered when the worker feels trusted to self-evaluate and continuously improve.

5. Once a manager establishes trust with a worker, then the movement toward quality has begun.

6. Without the gift of their creativity, workers cannot produce quality.

7. Lead Management also affects the bottom line in its reduction in medical expenses, absenteeism, accidents, and work disruptions that often reflect dissatisfied workers.

PART II
Managing for Quality

Since you have read this far, you are probably wondering how Choice Theory® with its special approach to workers is utilized to improve your bottom line. Now I will explain how Lead Managers make the best managers because they understand and respect workers values, which enables them to foster the empowered relationships that create competitive, high quality products and services for a global economy.

To give you a taste of what is to come in Part 2, I challenge you to recall from your own professional experience that leader or supervisor who was the best at nurturing you to manifest your potential in the role you carried. I wager that this person achieved this by communicating in some form not just their respect for your special contribution but also respect your values and dreams. Check it out and then read on to uncover how to do the same thing for your workers.

Chapter Six

Lead Managers Make the Best Managers

If one blind man leads another, both will end up in a pit.
—Matthew 15:14 The New American Bible

At the cafeteria at Jerri Inc. Gene commented to Anne about their CEO,

Frank expects me to give my best to the organization. But why would I if after 10 years, I still don't think he is in my corner.

Our workplaces stumble because of a bossing management tradition. Bosses are in charge of the workers. They tell workers when, and how to do their jobs. They have the authority to reward them for doing a good job or punish them for not doing so.

If workers have no union or civil service protection, not only their economic future, but also their well being could be in their boss's hands. Unfortunately, the unwise use of this authority effectively prevents us from achieving the quality work needed to attain a competitive place in our target markets.

Workers do not usually trust bosses because of the authority differential. If they are to expend both the mental and physical effort necessary to achieve quality work, managers need to stop bossing and to do all they can to establish a trusting relationship with the workers. This means moving beyond just the Behavioral and Strategy levels of communication.

In this context, trust means that the workers, based on experience, have come to believe that the manager has their best interests in mind. In other words the workers have learned, developed a belief, that their manager values them, their roles, and their work. To establish this trust, the manager needs to learn first to display respect and support and to give up the traditional boss prerogatives of criticizing and coercing the workers. Warren Bennis, in his best seller, *On Becoming a Leader* drives this point when he says, "You can't release the brain power of any organization by using whips and chains. You get the best out of people by empowering them, supporting them, and by getting out of their way."[7]

Therefore, what managers need to do to achieve quality is to give up bossing or Boss Management and start leading or using Lead Management. Adopting Lead Management means moving beyond the behavioral and strategy levels to include the beliefs, identity, and spirit levels. Let us begin by explaining Boss Management. It is quite simple. Reduced to its essentials, it contains four elements:

[1] The boss sets the task and the standards for what the workers are to do, usually without consulting the workers. Bosses do not compromise. Instead, the worker has to adjust to the job as the boss defines it or suffer the consequences as determined by the boss.

[2] The boss usually tells rather than shows the workers the task and rarely asks for their input as to improving the product or service.

[3] The boss, or someone he designates, inspects the work. Because the boss does not involve the workers in this evaluation, the workers only do enough to get by. They rarely even think of doing what is required for quality and efficiency.

[4] The boss uses coercion and punishment to try to make any resistant worker do the task their way. In so doing, the boss creates a workplace in which the workers and managers are adversaries. Bosses think that this adversarial situation is inevitable and the way it has to be to make a profit.

Boss-management is much more concerned with the agenda of the boss than that of the workers. Even so, many bosses have been able to see that Boss Management is so adversarial that it is counterproductive. We now have extensive research to prove that Boss Management is much less effective than Lead Management. There has been some softening of this hard-line, Boss Management, approach in some high tech and service industries where the educational and persuasive skills of the workers are paramount to the success of the company. Still much more needs doing beyond just softening the above description. We need to replace bossing with leading or we will not succeed in producing the quality we desire.

The worst feature of Boss Management is that it results in the workers and managers becoming adversaries. In fact, implicit in Boss Management is a denial of the three levels of thinking that are crucial to producing quality. Boss management negates the worker at the beliefs, identity, and spirit levels. Without communicating to workers at these levels, it is unlikely they will produce a quality product or service since they are not being valued for their whole self but rather just a small part—their Behaviors and Strategies. This lack of acknowledgement of their full being, the full range of how they experience their work, generates this adversarial relationship.

If this only occurred at the lowest level of an organization, it would be bad but not disastrous, since good design and engineering could make up for some of what the workers do not do. However, unfortunately, this adversarial relationship occurs at every level, and when it does, there is little chance for quality. Each boss-manager is more concerned with his own point of view than that of anyone else, and this low level of awareness prevents the cooperation that high caliber work requires.

This does not mean that all Boss Management is ineffective, but it is least effective where workers do not see the job as satisfying to them in all levels of their being. It is most effective where workers and boss have similar agendas and where the boss uses rewards more than punishments because rewards imply greater awareness of the other person's perspective. However, because it is not always ineffective does not in any way make it effective enough. It does not consistently produce the quality products and services we need.

As Bennis and Biederman pointed out,

> The standard models, especially the command-and-control style, simply will not work. The heads of great groups needs to act decisively but never arbitrarily. They have to make decisions without limiting the perceived autonomy of the other participants. Devising and maintaining an atmosphere in which others can put a dent in the universe is the leader's creative act.[8]

The key to change is an understanding of our managers and their managers about what it means to be a good manager. Two things are always on the mind of Lead Managers:

> [1] A manager is responsible for consistency of purpose and continuity in the organization. The manager is solely responsible to see that there is a future for the workers. This is, of course, important to the workers' beliefs, Identity, and Spirit. Moreover, no matter what the boss says, it is what he does that convinces or fails to convince the workers that he is concerned about their future.
>
> [2] The workers work in the system. The managers, in contrast, work on the system to see that it produces the highest quality product at the lowest possible cost. The distinction is crucial and bears repeating. *The workers work in the system while the manager works on the system.* No one else, only the manager, is responsible for the system as a whole and for improving it. Therefore, only the manager can initiate the change to communicating at all levels of the hierarchy rather than just the bottom two levels.

For workers to put the effort into the job that is necessary for quality work, they must be convinced, they must believe, that there is a future for them on the job, which enables them to tie their job to their beliefs, identity, and spirit. It is the same as trying to convince a tenant to take good care of a rental property. If he believes that he can live there at a fair rent for as long as he wants, he will take far better care of the property than if he knows eviction will come along as soon as some else will pay a little more.

Lead Managers are open and above board. They care about their workers. They are often not just colleagues but also friends and neighbors. Lead Managers already know how their job links to their own beliefs, identity, and spirit. They take pride in being able to tell anyone who asks why they love their job and how it relates to their own identity and its connection to their own spirit or purpose. Lead Managers model this caring and level of thinking for the workers who are encouraged to do the same.

Townsend and Gebhardt in *Quality in Action* state it this way, "Love is what makes leadership work; it is what makes the difference between manipulating people and leading people. You cannot manipulate people into doing quality work."[9]

Lead Managers base their reputations on their intent to provide good pay for every employee as long as the company is making a reasonable return on its investment. They are willing to tell their employees in writing what a reasonable return is and what they can expect as their fair share of this return. This frees the workers to focus their knowledge and skills—strategies and behaviors—on producing quality in the workplace.

Lead Managers are not short sighted. They take the long view, knowing that it takes time and dedication to build trust among workers. They do not try to increase profits by cutting wages or reducing personnel, because they are aware that workers treated this way will reduce, not increase, the quality of their work because their belief in being valued is threatened and so, too, are their Identities and Spirits. Lead Managers know low quality work leads to reduced profits and or reduced viability of the organization that leads to wage cuts and or layoffs.

To be specific, the four statements that are parallel to the statements used to define Boss Management define Lead Management:

[1] Lead Managers engage the workers in an ongoing, honest discussion of both the cost and the quality of the work needed for the company to be successful. They not only listen, but also encourage their workers to give them any input that will improve quality and lower costs. For example, Frank, the CEO at Jerri Inc. might ask Anne and Gene, "How do you think we can improve our product image over last year?"

[2] The Lead Manager, or his designate, shows or models the job so that the worker who is to do the job can see exactly what the manager expects. The Lead Manager works to increase the worker's sense of control over the work she does. For example, at the Millennium Community Hospital, Marie could say to Ray, her new Assistant Director, "Would you shadow me all this week so you can get a sense of our service delivery standards? We can then discuss how you think it can be enhanced."

[3] The Lead Manager eliminates most inspectors and inspections. He or she teaches the workers to inspect or evaluate their own work for quality with the understanding that they know a great deal, almost always more than anyone else, about what high quality work is and how to produce it economically. At Dave's Gas & Grocery, Dave might say to Raymond, "How do you think we can improve our staff scheduling over the vacation period this year, given your experiences last year?"

[4] The Lead Manager continually teaches and models for the workers that the essence of quality is constant improvement. To help them, he makes it

clear that he believes his main job is as a facilitator, which means he is doing all he can to provide them with the best tools and workplace as well as a respectful, supportive, non-coercive, non-adversarial atmosphere in which to work. As an example, at her weekly meeting, Jackie could say to her community health team, "While our results are good, I am wondering if our voice mail system needs a review and if anyone has noticed any other ways that we might improve our turn around time from first contact to service delivery?" (See Figure 2.2)

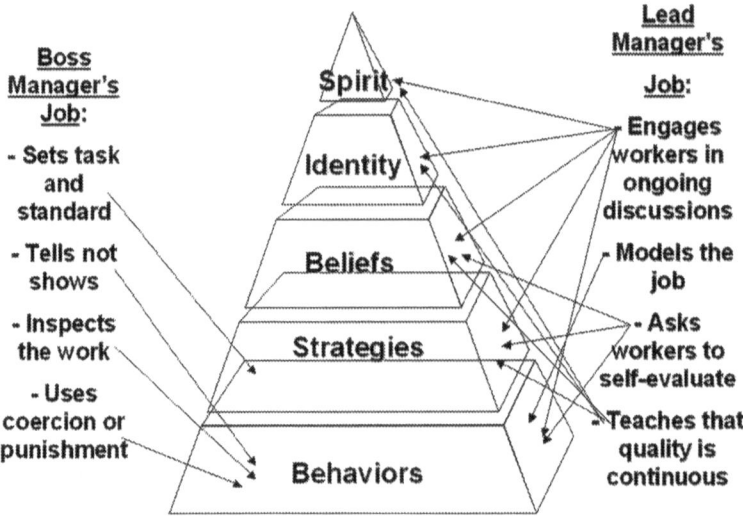

Figure 2.2 The Differences That Make the Difference

What is most difficult for boss-managers to realize is that the system itself creates the problem. Their tendency is to blame the workers, but the fault is not with the workers, it is with the system. Aguayo in referring to the work of Edward Deming and Joseph Juran, emphasized this point when he noted, "... in any system approaching stability, the bulk of the problems are due to the system, and that is the management's responsibility."[10] In addition, with this accountability for the system and the authority to act decisively within the organization, the relationship with the worker is the ultimate responsibility of the manager.

Therefore, relationships are the secret to producing quality in any form. We have known this about quality for a long time. Think of excellence in the military. The relationships built by leaders like Napoleon and Churchill with their followers characterize their success. We have also known this on the sports field. It is for this reason that we revere coaches who can build a team that will excel in performance. It is not surprising that similar principles apply in other organizations, created to achieve a goal with efficiency and quality. The difference today is in the level of thinking required by all concerned. Competing in the modern, technological economy demands higher and more complex levels of, not just behaviors, but also thinking. Quality only comes from people who are consciously purposeful in their work and led by managers who are able to nurture them at all levels of their thinking.

To be effective, managers must know a lot more than they do now about quality and what workers need and value to achieve it. So let us look at that next.

Seven Key Chapter Points

1. Workers need to perceive that their leaders value them in order to produce quality work.

2. Lead Managers need to be able to communicate at all five levels of their workers being to foster quality.

3. Workers work in the system to create quality while leaders work on the system to ensure it occurs.

4. Lead Managers operate at all five levels of being in their own work.

5. Lead Managers know that low quality is what destroys organizations.

6. Lead Managers talk about quality constantly, asks workers to evaluate their own work, and model continuous improvement.

7. Lead Managers know that problems are usually in the system not in the people.

Chapter Seven

Lead Managers Understand a Worker's Values

*What a man wants is simply independent choice, whatever that indepen-
dence may cost and wherever it may lead.*

—Fyodor Dostoevsky

Joe said to Rose after the weekly staff meeting of Dave's Gas & Grocery,

This comment touches the core of what is Lead Management. We have used the phrase, "managing people for quality" a great deal, but have not defined either management or quality. Now is the time to define these terms. We will not take anything for granted so that there is no doubt in the reader's mind as to what we are saying. Let us start with the most basic concept, quality.

A Definition of *Quality*

Managers need to be aware of the fact that quality is the constant core of what we all want, quality products and services at an affordable, though not necessarily lowest, price. One could say that the purpose of every organization is to produce a quality product or service at a marketable price. Therefore, quality is the key to competing successfully in any endeavor.

Quality is not definable if we are looking for a definition on which everyone will agree. It is, however, easily definable in the sense that each of us always knows what it is for ourselves. However, even without a precise definition, there is usually a great deal of agreement among consumers as to what constitutes quality. For example, if a specific brand and style of automobile was the best selling vehicle in its class, then we can assume that many people agreed it was a quality product. If a restaurant is prospering, it is likely that it is providing quality food and service at a fair price. If a senior's home care service is valued by its recipients; possesses skilled, dedicated staffed who display high morale and low absenteeism; and it operates within its policies and budget, then it is likely to be considered a quality public service agency.

Quality lasts. It is not faddish, and it is always useful. You can build a low-quality product that looks good and sells well for a while, but when people discover that it is not very useful, or it falls apart, they will stop buying it, even if it is cheap. Quality suffers if it remains the same. Maintaining it requires a continual effort to improve it, though, generally, the change will be gradual. The only thing that continues to improve with time alone is an antique. Some might say what makes an antique valuable is its intrinsic quality, which has lasted over time. Therefore, in a sense, every organization's desire is to become an antique. This is why a successful company will often tout the year of its conception, i.e. "Serving You Since 1947!"

Once customers decide that something is quality, they rarely change their minds. People tend to be loyal to quality. It may take quite a while for cautious customers to decide what quality is, but once they make up their minds that a product or service is quality, they will be reluctant to change that opinion. The product or service has to be very bad for a long time before a loyal customer will give up on it.

Once a customer changes his mind and decides that a product is no longer quality, then it is very hard to get that person to change his mind back to where it was. Any business doing well through its ability to offer a quality product or service and that wants to continue to prosper should have only one goal in mind: continually improve the product or service and, at the same time, try to maintain or even lower the price. And customers who realize that this is what a business is doing will be loyal through thick and thin because the customer has tied the product or service in some important way to several levels of their own Hierarchy of Being. For example, when I think about my Japanese vehicle which I purchased second hand nine years ago, I feel proud because I connect it to a quality product at my behavioral [it is easy and safe to drive] and strategy [I got it for a good price] levels, but also at other higher levels. At the belief level I am convinced I will save money in the long run, at the identity level I see myself as an astute shopper, and at the spirit level it reaffirms my commitment to the natural environment. I am a loyal Nissan customer even though its vehicles are often more expensive, and the interest rates are higher than many of their competitors. (See Figure 7.1.)

Figure 7.1 Levels of Thinking about a Quality Vehicle

The Three Conditions for Quality

Lead Managers understand that three basic conditions are required if the workers they manage are to do quality work. If the Lead Manager establishes these three conditions then two other conditions will emerge it ways that will surprise everyone. The three conditions for quality are:

Condition # 1 The work environment needs to be respectful, warm, and supportive with managers who are trusted.

Although we have already mentioned this earlier, it is so important that it needs repeating here. If workers are to do quality work, they must believe that the managers care about their welfare and all five levels of their being. We are talking, here, about trust. Trust is the belief that the person you trust not only will not hurt you but also, at all times has your welfare in mind. That is, the workers believe that the manager sees them as essential to the company's future. Warren Bennis says it this ways, "The manager relies on control, the leader on trust …"[11]

Workers need to be assured that their jobs are safe, that the company cares enough about them to treat them well and is willing to give them what they believe are not only fair wages but also a fair share of profits that have been earned through their quality labor. In the public sector, this translates into a fair wage for the responsibilities and duties involved that is comparable to a position in the private sector and recognition for the contribution they make to the community in which they work.

Above all, managers need to avoid trying to coerce workers with threats of punishment or offers of rewards that are beyond the usual fair pay and fair share of the profits. Quality disappears where there is coercion or when there is antagonism between the workers and the managers or among the workers. Rewards not offered to all workers tend to divide them and create antagonisms highly destructive to quality.

Managers need to do everything they can to encourage cooperation between managers and workers and among workers. Workers offer suggested solutions to production or service problems. This cannot be a token effort. Lead Managers ensure that the workers know that if they suggest something it is seriously considered. Townsend and Gebhardt reinforce this view when they point out "Trust is conveyed to employees in everyday behavior. It is not enough to say you trust someone, you have to demonstrate it."[12]

For example, at his manufacturing plant, Frank, who has heard from a customer about a flaw in one of their new products, might approach Anne with his concern by saying, "Anne, one of our customer's has pointed out a flaw in our new relay component. Would you set up a team meeting ASAP so we can brainstorm how to correct it?"

On the other hand, Marie, as a hospital administrator with a service complaint, might approach her team leader with, "Raymond, I have received a couple of complaints about the dietetic service fees. Can I get some time at your next team meeting so we can put our heads together and find a way address this issue?"

Lead Managers need to make a concerted effort to keep workers updated on any suggestion they make for enhancing quality. Workers treated in this way will produce far beyond what management expects. Genuine manager-worker and worker-worker cooperation in Lead Managed workplaces far exceeds that found in boss-managed workplaces. Townsend and Gebhardt say, "Leadership for quality must be active, obvious and informed."[13]

Condition # 2 Workers do only useful work and are encouraged to contribute to the usefulness of all work done.

Since quality is always useful, managers do not ask workers to do anything that is not useful. This does not mean that the usefulness of what the worker does needs to be immediately apparent. However, it is the manager's responsibility to explain the job, so that in a reasonable amount of time, the worker is able to see its usefulness and its link to his own Hierarchy of Being.

A Lead Manager would not say, "Don't bother me with questions, just do it!" A Lead Manager encourages a worker to question the usefulness of what she does and to give her opinion on how to improve the quality of the work.

Nothing destroys quality more than asking workers to do things that they do not believe are useful or refusing to listen to their ideas on how to make things better. From the worker's perspective, it is the same as denying them the strategies, beliefs, identity, and spirit of their being. In the military, punishment once consisted of digging holes and then filling them in again. It intend is obvious, to de-mean members—to take the meaning out of their being. To the extent that this goes on in business, it is destructive to quality. Unfortunately, this useless work is more the result of thoughtlessness than the desire to punish. Moreover, even though it has no punitive intent, its interpretation as a lack of caring or awareness, both impede quality products and services.

Condition # 3 Managers expect every worker to evaluate his or her work continually and to look for ways to improve it.

From the time workers are hired, Lead Managers will guide the process and help them to learn to evaluate their work continuously. Then, based on this ongoing self-evaluation, Lead Managers will encourage workers to improve the quality of what they do. For bosses, this will be the most difficult condition to implement. Bosses are so used to setting standards and then evaluating the worker's progress towards those standards that asking them to make this change is asking a great deal. However, a quality product or service is rarely the result of the evaluation of others rather it is usually the result of self-evaluation and continual improvement.

The traditional format of an inspector who inspects then passes or rejects the work is static and does not involve the worker. It will lead to passable, even periodic good work, but very little quality. Treated this way, workers will rarely do what they are capable of doing. Implied in this approach is an assumption of mistrust in the workers or their abilities to do the job at hand.

The idea that quality is conformance to standards is only useful if the workers have a role in setting the standards. In addition, they need encouragement to treat these standards as temporary. The only reason to stop trying to improve is if to continue to try is no longer cost effective. Managers, however, should not jump quickly to the conclusion that an improvement is not cost effective. It might be highly cost effective in terms of increasing market share, because quality is the key to market share and market share is the key to long-term success. Just ask the automotive industry.

Getting rid of the inspectors in a plant and letting, the workers (with some training, mostly from each other) inspect their own work saves substantial money. Since it ensures that there will be constant improvements, it is almost the only way to quality. When others evaluate workers and their work, the stage is set for the workers to spend their time and energy evaluating the evaluators and trying to figure out how to do as little as they can. This is a distraction to the workers since it wastes time and energy, taking it away from evaluating and improving what they do.

Applying these three conditions consistently, with respect and fairness, results in the emergence rather quickly of two effects. First, workers offer their employer their energy, creativity, and commitment, which results in them producing their best effort on the job. Second, both managers and workers experience feelings of personal balance and purposefulness about themselves, each other, and the work.

With the workers supported by respectful and friendly managers who listen to their suggestions, and with them evaluating their own work and contributing to improving the quality of the work, then quality products and services appear. As well, both the workers and the managers experience feelings of balance, satisfaction, and progress—all in the upper levels of the Hierarchy of Being.

In fact, assuming we do not use addictive drugs, we only feel balanced and well if we can introduce quality into our lives. The good feeling is neither the cause nor the result of the quality work. It is what we feel when we do anything that gets us involved with quality which reflects the upper levels of our own Hierarchy of Being.

This balanced centeredness becomes a powerful incentive for workers to want to continue to do quality work so that they can experience the purposeful feeling again. In addition, as quality becomes the norm, the manager feels the same way and has the incentive to continue to integrate the conditions of quality into her management.

The Definition of Lead Management

The three conditions of quality management apply in all instances of organizational life whatever form it takes. Therefore, Lead Management can also be described as the skill to persuade workers (without threats or coercion) to accept the manager's agenda; work hard at it and do a quality job.

Sometimes in public service agencies and small business there is less awareness of the need to be concerned with the skill and art of managing. However, Lead Management needs consideration in these sectors just as much as in the private sector. In fact, Lead Management first appeared in a book titled *The Quality School*. Its author, Dr. William Glasser, applied Lead Management to managing teachers and students. Lead Management warrants the attention of all other public sector areas where the profit factor is the conservation of taxpayers' money.

As a small business manager, you will need to expand the earlier description of Lead Management to include the skill of managing the workers so that they produce a quality product or service at a cost competitive enough so that the company assures itself a fair profit on its investment. Since all the people in the company are dependent for their livelihood on the company making a fair profit, quality work is the only way to assure long-run profitability and thereby company viability.

In most cases, the workers in public agencies have little direct financial incentive to do quality work, for example, to ensure that they will keep their jobs. However, a look at the three conditions of quality shows that financial incentives are only part of the first condition; they are not as important as we think. Research has demonstrated repeatedly that external factors such as wages and benefits, while important, are way down the list compared to internal motivators such as being valued, contributing, and having good leadership. The psychological incentives of being trusted, feeling useful, and being valued far outweigh the monetary benefits as long as they are fair.[14]

Very large companies are similar to public agencies in that a high-level manager, even a CEO, may continue to draw large salaries while the company is losing huge sums of money by providing poor service or products. In many organizations, private and public, there is a substantial lag between the failure of top managers to manage effectively and the suffering of any financial consequences for that failure. Boss-managed workers penalized by salary cuts or freezes or layoffs threats become incensed when top managers get raises or huge salaries while the organization is losing money. Angry workers will not do the quality work that is necessary if the company is again to become viable.

One need only check the business section of any major newspaper to find companies under scrutiny and hemorrhaging because the managers have been taking too much and the workers getting too little. The relationship of trust, where the workers feel betrayed, often becomes the focus of the media coverage. This is only logical since it is, as I stated earlier, in the relationship that lays the foundation for quality. Let us consider this relationship in detail next.

Seven Key Chapter Points

1. Quality is the key to competing successfully in any enterprise.

2. Warm, respectful, and trusting relationships with the workers are critical to the financial bottom line.

3. Every worker is an expert in his or her job and the improvements it needs for quality.

4. One of the best tools for continuous improvement is self-evaluation by the workers.

5. Lead Management frees the worker's energy, creativity, and commitment for the work.

6. A Lead Management approach ensures that both the leader and the worker gain more appreciation of self, their work, and their life.

7. Lead Managers have proven to themselves that this approach creates quality relationships in the workplace.

Chapter Eight

Empowered Relationships Create Quality

Ah well! I am their leader; I really had to follow them!

—Alexandre Auguste Ledru-Rollin

Jacqueline commented to Raymond over coffee in the hospital cafeteria,

Jacqueline has captured a key piece of what quality and Lead Management is all about. Quality products and services arise from quality relationships developed through trust. In this chapter, we will consider the ways you build trust in a quality-committed organization by focusing on the two ways that managers relate to workers.

Managing workers is about supervising, sharing information, and modeling skills to enhance the efficient completion of the task. However, a Lead Manager relates other crucial ways to their workers. A Lead Manager also relates as a friend and sometimes a coach who offers other perspectives on the world.

While we have so far limited our explanations of Lead Managing to the manager-worker relationship, Lead Managers must also learn to relate effectively as both a friend and coach. In this chapter, we will explain these other relationships because the more a manager is able to add them to his managing skills, the easier it becomes to manage.

Lead Manager as Friend

Friends are people who enjoy each other's company because they share interests and values. Work is, for most adults, the most common interest they share with each other. It is almost impossible to meet another human being without asking the question, "What do you do?" Most adults make many of their friends through work.

Many managers expect not to become friends with workers because they believe that workers may take advantage of this friendship. However, most managers have found that if they are friendly, it is easier to persuade workers to work hard and do a good job. Lead Managers find that as long as they take a friendly interest in what the workers are doing, asking them only to do useful work and to evaluate what they do, workers will not take advantage of their relationship. They will work much harder than if the manager is aloof or unfriendly.

Lead Managers are aware that friends will do more for each other than strangers. Thus, it is important not to ask so much that the worker believes that the manager is taking advantage of the relationship. The best approach is to discuss the situation and ask for input. For example, Gene, as a Lead Manager at Jerri Inc. might say to his team, "I realize that you are each anxious to get home today at your regular time. However, we need to fill all these orders before we quit for the day and I need your help. Our customers require them by morning. How do you suggest we could go about it?"

What this illustrates is that how you ask friends to work hard is often more important than what it is you are asking them to do. People are capable of doing prodigious amounts of work if they believe managers appreciate their knowledge and skills and they are involved in making decisions about their work. Making demands will rarely produce much work and it will never produce quality work.

If there were an axiom to friendship, it would be; the better we know and like someone, the more we want to and even enjoy doing things for them. Acting on this axiom, Lead Managers would reveal much more about themselves than traditional managers usually do. What they are actually doing is sharing the various levels of their own Hierarchy of Being so that their workers can see them as real people with similar challenges and aspirations.

What follows is a list of what I recommend you can do to accomplish this. This list is specific, but suggestions need to be specific to be effective. Take your time going through the list, doing only as much as you are comfortable doing. If you try too hard too fast, people you manage may interpret what you are doing as overselling and may doubt your sincerity. Because they are not used to this "let's get to know each other" approach, they may interpret too much effort on your part as coercive and you will be come less effective. It is also wise if you integrate these suggestions into the ordinary routine of your work. Occasions will arise when covering this or that point on the list will be natural and easy and you need to take advantage of these opportunities.

What we recommend may seem excessive at first, partly because few people who have managed you have ever done anything close to what I am suggesting. However, some have, and these managers you have worked for the hardest. This has certainly been the case for me. (See Figure 8.1.)

Figure 8.1 Lead Manager as a Friend

If you take your time, you will find that these suggestions are very enjoyable to implement and, in a quality workplace, it is very important that you enjoy the people you work with. As your people get to know you, they will in turn, reveal more about themselves. You and they will gain much of the closeness needed to satisfy the first condition of quality: a warm and friendly workplace.

When a natural opportunity arises, share the following with the people you manage:

a. Who you are.

b. What you stand for.

c. What you will ask them to do.

d. What you will not ask them to do.

e. What you will do for them and with them.

f. What you will not do for and with them.

Also, feel free to add to this list anything you believe will increase what you and your workers know and value about each other. Let us review each item on our list and explain why each is important.

A.   Who You Are

People usually have very specific opinions about who they are, why they are here, where they came from, and where they are going. People base their answers to these questions on a variety of sources that include their life experiences, values, religion, politics, hobbies, and interests. Moreover, because we need people so much if we are to satisfy our own needs, we are usually very curious about each other's past, values, opinions and interests. One thing we like about television is that we get to see and hear information about people that would usually be impossible to access. Moreover, if someone we know is on television, we make an extra effort to see that program.

For example, suppose you worked at the Millennium Community Hospital and Marie was your Director and she appeared on local television. Would you not make an effort to hear what she had to say? Further, suppose she spoke about herself at the Beliefs, Identity, and Spirit levels of her Hierarchy of Being. Suppose she revealed something about her life that you did not suspect—that as a twenty-year-old she had been a turned on, tuned out hippie. Then she explained how she decided to change her focus, to be more purposeful in her life.

Even if you did not report directly for her, if you liked what she said, could your relationship with her and with the organization be enhanced to some extent? Would you respect the CEO a little more for having overcome early challenges? Would you listen to her more attentively when she dealt with a company problem that affected you? Would she become a little more human to you than she was before? Sophisticated as you may be, you would still appreciate learning things you did not know about a person as important to you as she is.

Most of us know very little about other people except those with whom we live. While you are very important to those you manage, as a human being, you may be a complete mystery. Not knowing the facts, they may fantasize and build a false image of you based on little real information. As dull as they may be to you, people are interested in mundane statistics such as your age, martial status, whether you have children, whether you have a mother, father, or grandparents in your life, whether you live in a house or an apartment, and what kind of car you drive. They want to know about your interests: what you have done besides your current job, your favorite television programs, what music you like, what foods you prefer, and what things you dislike. The list could go on and on, but if you do not make your stories too long, they will be quite interested in what goes on in the other areas of your Hierarchy of Being. This enables them to find shared values, which makes it easier to build trust.

B.   What you stand for

Most interesting to all of us, and usually totally unknown to most of the people you manage, is what you stand for, what you believe is important in your work, in your community, and in the world. In essence, what are your values? Do you attempt to practice what you preach and how difficult is it for you? Do you have a stand on what is going on in the world, and what would you do about it if you had an opportunity? Are you involved in your community and, if so, how? This list could also go on and on, but what you stand for and why you stand for it is of endless interest to those who work for you.

For example, if you were one of Frank's staff at Jerri Inc. and you learned that after high school he had spent a year overseas in an under-developed country doing volunteer work, wouldn't that enhance your understanding of him and your ability to work with him?

If the people you manage respect you—and respect comes from a satisfying knowledge as well as good treatment—you can have a powerful impact on them. You may help them form opinions that will be supportive of the work they are doing. For example, you may help them understand why making the effort to treat a difficult customer well will pay off in the end.

In some instances, you may be the first person of your status who they have ever known much about. Not knowing people like you, they may form their opinions with insufficient information or information from biased or uninformed people. To help them form more accurate opinions, they need to find out what you value and why.

Finally, it is important to explain to the people you manage, and re-explain as the situation arises, that you will both support and challenge them. At the same time, you will not disrespect them or put them down. Explain that disrespect and put-downs cause much of the friction that makes it difficult for quality work to flourish. Quality comes from a balance of support and challenge inside a respectful relationship. There is no other way.

C.   What You Will Ask Them to Do

In a quality-focused organization, you need to make sure workers know what you will ask them to do. Telling them what you will ask them to do is meaningless if you do not model it yourself. For example, if you ask them to be on time and ready to go to work, then you must first demonstrate it by being on time and ready for work. If you tell them this is the rule from now on, then it must be the rule: no exceptions for the people who have more authority. So, for example, if Marie has lunch with Jackie, she respects the allotted lunchtime of one hour since she is aware she is a model for her colleague and everyone else in the hospital.

In a quality-focused organization, although you will not put anyone down, you need to tell your workers this does not mean you will not handle problems. Tell them you are going to ask them to work with you to solve any problems that arise no matter how small. You will ask them to do this as individuals, in small groups, or even in large groups if there is a big problem affecting everyone. You are probably much more interested in them solving their own problems than in you doing it for them. You should encourage them to get together without you and then discuss the results with you.

D.   What You Will Not Ask Them to Do

Considering that most of your workers will come from boss-managed organizations, explain that in a quality-focused organization you will no longer ask them to be subservient or to do things just because you say so. You want them to speak up and suggest how to do the job better, not to keep quiet. Also, explain that you are not going to ask them to do anything useless and, if they think a certain practice or procedure is useless, they should be sure to discuss it with you.

E.   What You Will Do for Them or with Them

In a quality-focused workplace, workers will want to make an effort to learn and improve, so you will make it clear to them that you are available to help them in any way you can or, if possible, in any way they want. You are their friend, you are always on their side, and it will never be you against them. For example, if they need more time to figure something out or to do a better job, you will give it to them, advise them on where to get help, or take off your coat, roll up your sleeves, and pitch in. If they have questions, you will either answer them or find someone who can. If they have an idea about how to make things better, you will take the time to listen to them. They are doing the work; you are doing all you can to support them.

At the same time, tell your workers you are not perfect, and, if they find you are not doing as you say, they are free to tell you and you will explain your thinking and adjust as required. Also, tell them that when problems arise on the job, you will ask them for help and you welcome their ideas. Show them you value their ideas. Show them you value their help by getting together with a small group of workers and asking them to brainstorm solutions. This shows that you believe in cooperation, and it encourages them to work together to solve problems. In some cases, it encourages them to solve their problems without even telling you what they are.

F.   What You Will Not Do for Them

You will not do their work or solve the problems they should solve themselves. You will not tell them what to do unless it is obvious that they need direct help. Mostly, you will tell them that quality comes from their figuring out, not from you telling them, what to do.

If a new worker is unclear about the differences between your roles, you can sit with that worker for a few minutes and, in a friendly discussion, complete the Role-Clarification Matrix presented in Figure 8.2. It is a simple and practical way to help everyone understand your Lead Management approach. It takes only a few minutes and helps to build and maintain a trusting relationship with your worker.

You communicate that you are their leader, not their boss. More and more you will stop evaluating their work and turn this job over to them. If they ask you for an opinion, you will give it, but not unless they are also willing to express their opinions and defend them. Explain that to be successful in life, we must evaluate ourselves and work to improve. We cannot and should not depend on others to do this for us.

The Lead-Manager's Job is to:	The Worker's Job is to:
Provide Leadership Provide a friendly workplace Provide materials and tools Provide fair compensation Listen to Worker's suggestions Etc.	Work hard Evaluate their own work for quality Suggest ways to improve the work Cooperate with others Be punctual Etc.
The Lead-Manager's Job is Not to:	**The Worker's Job is not to:**
Disrespect worker's values Criticize worker's performance Be late for work Evaluate worker's product Threaten the workers Etc.	Disrespect leader's values Ignore safety procedures Be late for work Evaluate colleague's work Criticize colleagues Etc.

Figure 8.2 Role-Clarification Matrix

Lead Managers Avoid Seven Behaviors That Destroy Relationships

The seven behaviors that people commonly do that are destructive to relationships are:

a. Criticizing

b. Blaming

c. Threatening

d. Bribing

e. Punishing

f. Complaining

g. Nagging

Even strong relationships like marriages, family ties, lifelong friendships, and business partnerships many flounder when one of the people starts to use one or more of these behaviors. If one or more of these behaviors can shatter very close relationships, they can undermine the more fragile relationships that exist between managers and workers. When you consider a worker's Hierarchy of Being, it becomes clear how these seven behaviors would disrespect it in the workplace. Moreover, of the seven, the first two, criticizing and blaming, even if the manager believes it is justified or constructive, are probably the most harmful. Coercion, which includes the next three of threatening, bribing, and punishing, is almost as bad. The last two primarily encourage people to avoid you.

The first thing a successful manager learns is not to criticize or coerce. If this is all a manager learns, it is still a huge amount. Just refraining from criticizing or coercing will greatly increase your effectiveness as a Lead Manager. However, building relationships necessitates the use of seven caring behaviors, which are the antithesis of the ones mentioned earlier. These behaviors in the repertoires of Lead Managers form the foundation for all their relationship-building skills. We are all familiar with these behaviors since we use them regularly within the circles of our family and friends. However, Lead Managers take them to work and use them there to create the relationship required to create quality products and services. The seven caring behaviors are:

1. Accepting
2. Respecting
3. Trusting
4. Encouraging
5. Supporting
6. Listening
7. Negotiating

Albert Einstein said, "You are or become those things which you repeatedly do." So using the seven caring behaviors with your workers could turn them quickly into your habits and who you are, could they not?

Dr. John Demartini in his latest book, *The Heart of Love*, also emphasizes this point when he refers to three kinds of relationships: careless, careful, and caring.[15] Careless relationships occur when the manager asserts that his values are the right ones and the worker's are not important. This is a typical approach of a boss-manager, and it prevents the creation of quality. Careful relationships occur when the manager ignores his or her own values and gives priority to that of the worker. This also undermines the creation of quality as well as productivity. Caring relationships, the third kind, occur when the manager respects their own values and that of the worker and so inserts his values inside that of the worker to create quality products and services and bottom line success. Demartini offers its business application with, "Incidentally, what we call *caring* in a personal context, is called *selling* in business. To develop quality connections with others, you'll be required to master the art of conveying your value in terms of someone else's in order to demonstrate your affection in this special way."[16]

Lead Manager as Coach

A coach helps another person: the coached, who wants the help. The help is usually in the form of giving information or offering suggestions or perspectives. Having a coach is voluntary. If you are dealing with a person who is not doing well but does not want help, coaching will not work. This does not mean he or she cannot improve, but it is much more accurate to refer to that kind of help as managing rather than coaching.

A coach is working with a volunteer who wishes information, suggestions or perspectives while a manager is working with a paid employee who is performing a task. Lead Managers are clear about the difference between managing and coaching and are comfortable moving between the two roles as the situation demands. Lead Managers realize both roles have value in providing quality and yet they are distinct.

For example, you would coach a worker who came to you and asked for your perspective on how to deal with a work problem or personal problem. You would also coach a worker who asked you how to cope with another worker who was not cooperating in getting the work done. Managing, on the other hand, would be the situation in which you recognized that a worker was doing badly at work but refused your initial offer to coach him through the situation. Since the worker has refused to work with you in this coaching role, to do your job, and honor your own values, you will need to switch to a managerial role. Otherwise, it could jeopardize the quality of the product or service you are responsible for providing. An example might be a worker who is using illegal drugs to the point that his use interferes with work. On the other hand, it could be a worker has a grudge against another worker that affects the work, and this person has refused your invitations to discuss it in a coaching styled meeting, these would be candidates for managing not coaching.

What I will focus on here is how to coach workers who want help. Later, I will explain how to approach and manage workers who do not want help. Problems like these are very common and lead to great expense for the company. Moreover, a manager who is capable of handling them is a valuable asset. This aspect of managing is much more difficult than coaching.

Managers need to coach because workers or subordinates naturally look to their supervisor or team leader for advice and guidance in areas that have nothing to do with the job. In the case of Lead Managers, whom they trust, this could be frequent, and the willingness to offer brief, friendly coaching should be routine.

A variation of coaching that a Lead Manager should use frequently is to ask a worker for help with any sort of problem the manager notices. The worker who does the job knows more about it than anyone else, and there is no better way to tap his expertise than to ask the worker for advice on some aspect of what he knows and, then, take his advice.

Workers who find that their manager depends on them for advice will work hard with few complaints. The key is to ask for advice and then try very hard to take it. You need to use as much as you can and thank the worker for what he suggested. If applicable, also explain to the worker why only some of the advice was usable, and, from this honest discussion, the worker can learn more about the broader implications of the job. Keep in mind that when a worker learns that any of his advice was useful, that knowledge will spur him to work harder and quality will increase.

Managers need to get close to the most respected individual workers. These workers can assist other struggling workers. They can feel out another worker who is having a problem and offer help without the manager's direct intervention. If, however, the problem worker asks the helping worker, "Did the manager ask you to do this?" the helping worker needs to be truthful by revealing, "The manager thought a little help was needed and asked me to talk with you. If you want to find out more, he told me he is quite prepared to discuss it with you. He just wants to help too."

Managers need to anticipate difficulties and deal with them before they get serious. Quality relates directly to commitment and when workers are involved in giving advice to and getting it from managers whom they consider their friends, they tend to be loyal. Wellins, Byham, and Wilson in their work, *Empowered Teams*, capture the essence of this, "The key here is that super leaders encourage and coach others to internalize and self-manage much of the control that was previously imposed by supervisors and managers."[17]

In union shops, managers need to develop a great sensitivity to the relationships between themselves, the union leaders, and the workers. A person can be a union member and still be on friendly terms with the manager. What is important is that the manager does not take advantage of that relationship and coach a worker in a way that the manager's advice puts the worker into a conflict with the union.

The danger of giving advice is that it could be destructive to the friendship you are always trying to establish. If the advice is taken and does not work, the manager can get blamed. If the advice works, it can create an unhealthy, dependent relationship. What successful Lead Managers really do is offer the worker their perspective on a situation, what they have learned from their experiences. Information offered in this way, as a caring coach's perspective, is unlikely to be misinterpreted.

Even when the worker asks for advice, you need to be careful not to criticize him if he does not appreciate your perspective. There must be no coercion to adopt your perspective either. If this occurs, the distrust of the worker will be much more destructive than not offering the perspective at all. People who ask for help will often refuse good counsel, and managers need to be prepared to accept this fact of life.

Lead Manager as Teacher/Modeler

We mentioned that the role of a Lead Manager is to be a friend, coach, and manager. However, let us consider for a moment the important role of teacher and modeler. For an organization to achieve quality, it must function also as a learning organization—a school. The managers themselves will often be the teachers and models for the workers who are the learners. Moreover, this school must function far different from the ones most workers attended. In public school, the students try to get by far more than they try to learn because most of what they are learning has little or no connection to their values or apparent use in their lives. The diploma, however, can be quite useful.

A learning organization is the Lead Manager's milieu. Senge et al. in *The Fifth Discipline Fieldbook Strategies and Tools for Building a Learning Organization*, list some of the traits of a learning organization. It is a place where people feel they are doing something that has value, are growing and enhancing their capacity to create, are envisioning the enterprise from all angles and levels, are free to explore everyone's beliefs and values, experience mutual respect and trust, and feel free to experiment, take risks and openly assess the results.[18]

In the company school, the usefulness of everything workers learn should be either obvious or fully explained. In this school, the managers themselves must be prepared to teach and model, and, even more, they must train skilled workers to teach and model for other workers.

Quality is not a static thing so this educational requirement is continuous. Quality is the result of constantly improving the system, and the only way to do this is to learn better ways to do the job. Workers need to be encouraged to be constantly on the alert for better ways to do their job and to report to their manager when they think they have discovered something worthwhile.

Lead Managers give workers who make discoveries their attention and immediately start planning how to teach these improvements to all who could use them. If managers are not prepared to listen, the workers will not talk with them and are even likely to stop trying to improve what they are doing. A good teacher listens to her pupils, and by her modeling, they will then also listen to her.

In almost all instances, both the managers and the workers will perceive themselves to be products of schools that not only taught material of little practical value but also contained few teachers who listened to their students. They also often believe they attended schools where teachers used criticism and coercion to motivate students, and where only a handful of students worked hard and did quality work. In a quality-focused organization, such perceptions about learning need to be completely changed. In a quality-focused organization, the work must be quality and the workers need to learn to be quality focused, which also means the managers need to be Lead Managers who have the knowledge and skills to facilitate this process.

Unlike school, where students are tested mostly on what they can remember (almost all of which is quickly forgotten); only what is relevant to doing quality work should be taught on the job. The only test of what is learned is whether the learner applies it successfully to the job. Lead Managers measure success by the single criterion: Does it improve the quality of the work?

In a Lead-Managed organization, it would be the worker's evaluation of his own work that would determine whether the education led to improving the quality of the product or the service. Everything taught needs explaining and modeling, so that all the workers clearly understand that what they are learning relates to improving the quality of the work and the workplace. In so doing they also link it to their own Hierarchy of Being.

To function as a school, the organization needs to adopt a definition of education that is far different from how education was defined in the schools both managers and workers attended. In almost all schools, and even in a great many colleges and universities, education is defined as learning, usually memorizing, what the teacher teaches or face the consequence of low grades or failure. To get credit, students have to pass the test, but passing the test almost never indicates that the learning had anything to do with their values, usefulness or quality.

In a quality organization, education is the process through which the workers (as students) discover that learning adds quality to their lives. For a commercial organization, this definition extends to adding quality to the worker's lives and to the lives of the customers. Education would then become student-centered and, in the case of commercial organizations, customer-centered. Managers who accept their role as teacher and modelers and who are willing to define education as it is defined here are vitally needed if we are to have quality organizations that can survive in today's highly competitive, commercial world.

Seven Key Chapter Points

1. Only quality relationships can produce consistent quality products and services.

2. Lead Managers know that sharing their own Hierarchy of Being with their workers can build quality relationships.

3. Lead Managers know their responsibility to model what they expect from their workers.

4. Lead Managers are able to differentiate their roles from that of the worker.

5. Lead Managers avoid the seven deadly behaviors that sabotage relationships.

6. Lead Managers use the seven behaviors of caring communications.

7. Lead Managers are ready to coach and teach their workers, as the situation requires.

PART III
Putting It All Together

By this point, you might be thinking, "Lead Management is too soft; it bends too far in the direction of workers. I will lose so much authority that the workers won't respect me, and I won't have the power to act decisively when problems arise." If your company or organization has the market locked up, you can afford to think this way and this book is not for you. If, however, you are not in this situation, then your difficulty with Lead Management is not that it is too soft. It is that you find it difficult to conceptualize how much you have to do to achieve quality.

Consider an example of a quality product and service I experienced. Before she died, my mother-in-law, a prodigious knitter, would take the leftover ends of her yarn, and, matching them up, knit beautiful, one of a kind, multi-colored socks. In her memory, I decided to have one of each of the five pair that had worn out, framed in some way. I took them to an owner/operator of a local framing store with instructions to use his discretion to mount them in a frame.

When I returned to pick up my socks, the quality of his effort dazzled me. Inside a shadow box, he had created a clothes line with the each sock hung with an old-fashioned clothespin. In the background was a sun-lit field of potatoes with willowy clouds floating by. He created a work of art that has become a family heirloom. Several framing businesses around town offer good service. However, I only go to one place after the level of dazzling service I received. How could I go elsewhere?

This experience illustrates my point. I realize that dazzling service is hard to conceptualize, but this is exactly what every business that has a competitor must learn to do. This book is not addressed to those who want to be good enough, or a little better than before, in their level of quality. Customers and clients now expect good service and are willing to pay for it. However, even that is not enough. To be ahead of our competitors, to have a viable future, we will need to *dazzle* our customers if we want to stay at the leading edge of whatever product or service we offer the customer. If we, as managers, cannot persuade the people we manage to put our service or product into their quality worlds, our ability to compete will continue to decline.

We have overwhelming evidence that the losses and layoffs in prestigious companies come from the lack of creative improvements, which occurs when the top stops listening to those struggling at the cutting edge where buying, selling, and servicing takes place. Competitors who practice continuous improvement will race ahead. Customers take these troubled companies out of their quality worlds and, as business declines, these companies lay off workers to compete for price. But ruthless cost-cutting alienates the very workers who must be depended on to do the quality work, which is the only thing that can restore the competitiveness that has been lost. Some formerly great companies may not recover from this catch-22.

Semi-benevolent dictators who managed well enough in lightly competitive markets but could not compete when the competition got tough have run many of these companies. Today, we are mostly hiring in industries such as fast food where price rather than quality are the norm, but even here, as competition heats up, only the higher-quality companies will survive.

So now, let us bring these ideas together, put them into practice, and see what is possible with an enlightened Lead Management approach.

Chapter Nine

Quality Relationships Create Quality Products and Services

Unless you have a sense of values that are shared by people and turn them loose to do certain things on their own within those sets of values, the organization, whether a nation or corporation or citizen group, just doesn't work very well.

—Alan Cranston

At the annual Hospital Picnic Raymond, while taking his turn at the barbeque, blurted out to a Jacqueline,

Jacqueline, does Marie really think she can criticize me or my work and that I will then increase my effort after she implied I am incompetent?

So far, I have explained what a Lead Manager should do. Now I want to focus on what a Lead Manager should not do: criticize. No matter how badly an employee performs, it is unwise to criticize his or her performance. Difficult as it may be for you to accept, I do not believe that there is such a thing as constructive criticism. Criticism negates all levels of the Hierarchy of Being and eliminates the possibility of quality occurring in the workplace. See Figure 9.1 The Cost of Criticism.

Figure 9.1 The Cost of Criticism

This does not mean that the manager accepts poor performance or fails to deal with it. On the contrary, a Lead Manager does not let anything slide that she believes needs improvement. She deals with it as soon as she can, but she does so without using anything that the employee can reasonably construe as criticism. In fact, it would be good practice for all Lead Managers to post a sign in their workplace, with their signature prominently displayed at the bottom, stating something like the following:

My Problem-Solving Approach
In this department, I will attempt to help all employees solve their problems
that either they or I become aware of, but in so doing,
I will not criticize, put down or punish.
I encourage all employees to do the same with each other, and me.
Signed, _____

Criticism occurs in many direct and indirect forms, all of which reduce quality. Not only can it be verbal but it can also be a gesture, a tone of voice, a look of disdain, a refusal to talk with, listen, or see someone, or even an insincere attempt to deal with a problem. Criticism is anything an employee interprets as criticism, because that employee will act as if it were and quality will suffer.

I accept that it is very difficult for a manager, who sees a multitude of short-comings as he walks around, to do as suggested here. It seems so right to call the employee in and explain how much better he could do his job if he would do it the manager's way. This certainly does not seem to be critical, but even this will be interpreted by almost all employees as criticism. Even if they are aware they are doing something wrong, they will still resent the reminder, even if presented politely. In addition, they will channel that resentment into resistance, which means energy that could improve what they are doing redirects itself into resistance and, again, quality suffers. It is criticism from the manager that is the largest cause of energy-wasting, adversarial relationships that exist between many employees and boss-managers.

Choice Theory® explains clearly that none of us will put anyone who criticizes us, or what we do, into our quality worlds. We will not, because when criticized, accurately or not, we feel we have lost power, love or friendship, and the freedom to act as we think best. It is as simple as that. It does not matter that the criticism has justification or that, in private, the employee agrees he was doing something wrong.

This is never a question of right or wrong; it is a question of how the employee perceives the manager's actions and, from the employee's standpoint, he will perceive any criticism as a barrier to admitting both the manager and what the manager wants him to do into his quality world. To a Lead Manager, the most important thing he must do if he wants quality work is to treat the employees in such a way that he gains entrance into their quality worlds. To achieve this, he focuses on eliminating criticism from all he does with everyone in the company: subordinates, equals and superiors. It may be easier for you to understand what I am talking about if you think about how you would approach a superior whom you believed was doing something wrong. It is not likely that you would directly criticize him.

For example, Rose, a Team Leader at Dave's Gas & Grocery, who recently was upset because her regular shift suddenly changed without apparently any input from her, went into the owner's office and said to him, "Dave, I am confused by the change in my shift and was wondering if we could discuss what was decided." In so doing, Rose displayed a wise, Lead Management approach to a problem.

Lead Managers approach all employees who need to improve what they are doing in the same way. Therefore, Rose could say to one of her team something like, "It seems to me that there may be a problem here, and I would like to talk with you and see if we agree." The emphasis is on "we" not on you and me. Further, she might add, "If we agree there is a problem, we want to look at what each of us can do to solve it." If the employee does not see it as a problem, Rose needs to be ready to admit that there might not be a problem by saying, "Let's talk further. You may be right. I will be happy to agree if we find that no problem exists."

If the employee is willing to admit that there may be a problem, as most will, then Rose as our Lead Manager can say, "Let's see what each of us is doing that may be generating the problem." She does not say that it is all or even part of the employee's fault. In fact, as she talks to the employee, she will never even suggest it is anyone's fault. She will ignore the idea of fault altogether and emphasize from start to finish that all she is interested in is solving the problem. She is not even interested in the history of the problem unless that history is vital for its solution.

The Lead Manager is also willing to involve anyone else, even a whole team, in the solution to the problem. Often the employee will admit that there is a problem, but to avoid criticism he will not admit that he is at fault. The employee might suggest someone else is at fault. The Lead Manager will listen and then say," Okay, let's get that person involved. Will you help me explain what's wrong and what needs to be done to correct it?" She reemphasizes that she is not looking to criticize or find fault; all she is looking for is a way to solve the problem.

At the same time, the Lead Manager will caution an employee who has a lot to do with the problem but who wants to implicate more people that they may end up with a bigger problem than they have now. The purpose of this approach is to involve only the person who is most associated with the problem in solving it. To do this and avoid criticism, I suggest you say something like, "I think we can solve this. You know what the problem is, and you have many skills. Let's see if we can put it to rest without involving a lot of other people." This allows the employee to work on the problem in a way that he escapes blame and criticism. In doing so, he can put all his energy into solving it.

The Lead Manager is trying to set up a no-fault, no-criticism policy. Once this policy is set, the Lead Managed employees will tend to do much more evaluating than bossed employees do. It is not that the bossed employees do not evaluate, they do. However, what they evaluate is everything and everyone else but themselves. It is always someone else's fault, because in a boss-managed environment their main concern is to avoid blame and criticism.

In the non-blaming, non-criticizing Lead Management environment, they will feel free to evaluate their work, quality will increase, and they will solve problems by themselves without even going to the manager. In this trusting atmosphere, they will work together and, in doing so, will get away from the situation caused by criticizing and punishing in which each employee protects her own turf even if it is to the detriment of the company.

We realize this is a challenging thing to do. We live in an external control, blaming, criticizing, faultfinding, punishing society in which people find it very hard to trust each other. Cooperation is quality's foundation within the organization. For cooperation to exist there must be trust. It is only in this way that an organization is able to compete successfully with other organizations.

Seven Key Chapter Points

1. The intention of the manger is not relevant where criticism is concerned because criticism in any form prevents quality work.

2. Workers who perceive themselves as being criticized will not only not do quality work but will direct their genius elsewhere, often into some form of resistance.

3. Criticism can come in many forms including direct, indirect, verbal, or nonverbal.

4. Perceived criticism creates the adversarial relationship between mangers and workers.

5. Each worker is doing the best she or he can so any problem requires attention to a solution rather than to finding blame.

6. A "no fault and no criticism" approach is the most effective way to build and maintain the trust that is needed for quality.

7. Cooperation is the basis of quality, and trust is essential for it to occur.

Chapter Ten

Quality Environments Create Quality Products and Services

Modern man is the victim of the very instruments he values most. Every gain in power, every mastery of natural forces, every scientific addition to knowledge has proved potentially dangerous, because it has not been accompanied by equal gains in self-understanding and self-discipline.

—Lewis Mumford

At Dave's Gas & Grocery, Joe commented to Rose at the Annual Christmas Get Together,

Joe actually sat down with me and we discussed how we are going to meet next year's sales quotas. Rose, we came up with a good plan. It felt great to be included and listened to with respect. He sure has come a long way. He is a good guy to work with!

Managers who order workers about sabotage productivity in the workplace. Lead Managers soften this approach with the non-coercive technique of asking. To most employees there is an implication of coercion in telling that is absent in asking. As I help people learn the skills of Lead Managing, I find that, next to teaching self-evaluation, learning to supervise non-coercively, for example, by asking rather than telling, is the hardest part of the process. Fueled by a lifetime of exposure, starting in our homes, accelerating in our school, and peaking in many of our work experiences, coercion has become so ingrained that it is literally a part of what most of us consider to be common sense. Even though it is so destructive to the goal of quality, it seems so right.

For years I have been using and teaching this method of non-coercive counseling, called Reality Therapy, to thousands of people. Many of these people are business executives, public servants, and small business operators. Many others are counselors or educators who do not think of themselves as managers. It is obvious, however, that most of what teachers do is manage because, similar to business, they also have an agenda for their students and are trying to get them to accept this agenda. In the case of counselors, many of whom counsel delinquents or addicts, I have no difficulty teaching that coercion does not work. They accept the idea that they must persuade the people they counsel to put them in their quality worlds or their counseling will be ineffective.

When I work with teachers, it is apparent that students are much more difficult to manage successfully than people who work for a living. Most teachers are systemic boss-managers whose philosophy centers on coercion: behave and learn as I tell you or face low grades or failure. Students in school learn a variety of ways to resist this bossing, so when they leave school and go to work, they are well prepared to resist the threats and punishments that continue as a usual part of the work process.

Therefore, what I help both counselors and teachers learn is much more than counseling and teaching, it is how to manage successfully and it is fully applicable to business. In fact, less skill is required of business managers than of counselors and teachers because, unlike students, employees get paid and mostly see what they are asked to do as useful. Because of this, they tend to want to do a good job much more than a student wants to learn history or an alcoholic wants to stop drinking. Therefore, while both school and business require Lead Management, business is by far the easier place to put it in practice.

Creating the Lead Management Environment

Dealing with people non-coercively means making work a talking and listening place, especially listening. More than anything else, this helps the workers feel as if they have some power, and the more workers feel empowered, the more likely they are to do quality work. That workers who feel powerless will not do quality work is as logical as a straight line is the shortest distance between two points.

When managers talk with workers, they need to solicit their opinions on almost anything. Once the workers get the idea that the manager is interested in what they have to say, it will be natural for them to talk about the job and give their opinion on all aspects of what they are doing. As managers listen and talk with the workers, they should begin, as soon as possible, to bring up the subject of quality. Frequent and free discussions on quality related to the job need initiation by the manager.

Managers need to explain that they are now leading instead of bossing. For a long time, workers who have been bossed all their lives will tend to see even a relaxed, friendly, conversational manager as a boss. It takes time for them to realize that Lead Management is different from bossing. When a manager asks workers repeatedly, what he can do to help them to do a better job, and the manager does much of what the workers ask they will see that he practices what he advocates. As they do, they will become aware that this manager is very different from the usual boss.

Managers need to make clear that they do not criticize or punish. They accomplish this by avoiding these things and by talking with workers directly on the subject. Tell them straight out that, what we do is solve problems: we believe that criticism or punishment increases problems; it does not solve them. Lead Managers tell workers that they do not see them as adversaries, as people needing punishment to accomplish what the managers want. They drive this point home by not punishing workers in situations where, by tradition, punishment occurred.

For example, Raymond misses a day's work and expects to lose a day's pay or have to lie and use a day of sick leave. Marie, a Lead Manager knows the worker was not sick; it may have been the first day of hunting season or perhaps his aging parent has been ill. Instead of being critical or punitive, Marie asks Raymond if he can work out a way to make up the work or plan with her in the future so that Raymond can have a few special days. Marie continually emphasizes that her goal is quality work; she is not interested in chaining Raymond to the job if there is a more flexible way to get it done. She shows through this approach that Raymond's values and welfare are important to her. Marie must also honor her value of quality and productivity. However, with respect for her value evident, her flexibility manifests itself.

In non-union workplaces, Lead Managers take care of their workers by not wait for them to ask for a raise. As quality and production rise, the manager needs to approach all the workers individually and in small groups to explain the company wants to work out a way to share the profits achieved through their quality work. To demonstrate their good will, a statistical record of productivity and quality shows everyone the company's gains. Groups rather than individuals need rewards. Individual rewards should be limited to one-time bonuses for good suggestions. What this fair share may be is a subject for negotiations, but a Lead Manager would work out an agreement with the workers so that their pay connects to productivity and profits. Bosses do not do this. They use raises to coerce in ways that are often capricious and beyond the worker's control.

Finally, the Lead Manager emphasize regularly that the work quality must constantly improve. He is relentless in his conviction that his employees are as good as or better than any workers are. He demonstrates the idea that he does not give up no matter what problem arises. He is steadfast in his belief that there are solutions to almost anything. The work environment is a "we can do it" one where coercion does not appear.

Solving Problems with Counseling

The thrust of this whole book so far is to explain how Lead Managers create workplaces where serious problems are unlikely to arise. However, no matter how good a job they do, both work and personal problems will occur regularly. This is an organizational fact. To assure quality, these problems need attention. If the problems are work related, they need handling as soon as the Lead Manager becomes aware of them. Delay only makes things worse. If they are not directly work related, such as difficulties at home, drinking, drug abuse, or financial distress, it may be difficult to tell if an employee's work is affected. Since there is a good chance it is, the Lead Manager should also deal with these problems as time permits. In all of these situations, the manager just counsels, so learning to do this should be part of the preparation for Lead Managing.

Once Lead Managers develop a reputation for being capable of helping workers solve problems, the workers, having not experienced this kind of treatment before, will increasingly bring problems to them. However, they will realize that managers are not professional counselors and will not expect miracles. If they only listen sympathetically, workers will appreciate their effort and mark them as managers worthy of respect and hard work.

In this brief chapter, we cannot teach counseling, but we can offer you a simple and effective model for using the Lead Management principles. It is a series of five simple questions that can help any worker move from the frustration or despair of a personal problem to taking effective action to resolve it. Often a worker will feel overwhelmed by a personal problem. However, because of your relationship with him or her, as an inspired Lead Manager you can offer them direction and support by taking them for "A Walk in the Park." (See Figure 10.1.)

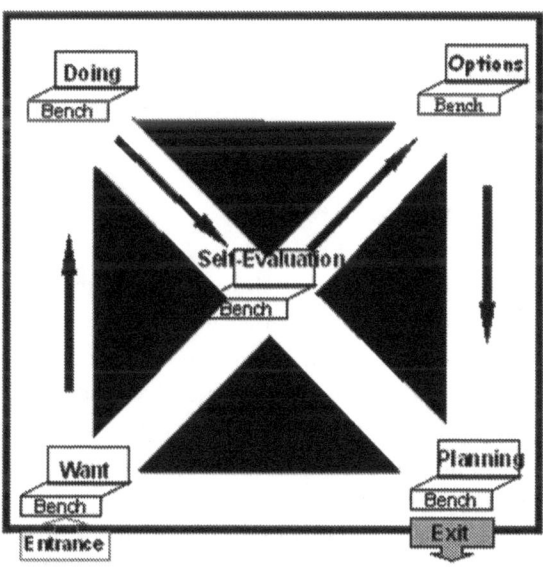

Figure 10.1 A Walk in the Park

"A Walk in the Park" is a simple, practical, problem-solving tool learned easily and used quickly by a Lead Manager. It's metaphor is a park I played in as a child. This makes an effective metaphor for applying Lead Management with a worker who is struggling. By following the *M shape* path and directions of the arrows and visiting, each bench in the park and its corresponding question the Lead Manager provides the worker with an opportunity to explore his problem with someone he already trusts. The Lead Manager acts only as the guardian of a journey through the park. The worker has an opportunity to analyze his problem with a supportive person who will encourage him to self-evaluate and identify a new course of action.

Let us consider each question independently. Notice how each one facilitates the worker taking control of her life and continuing to do her job. Each question comes from some aspect of Lead Management principles so there are no surprises in taking "A Walk in the Park." The five simple questions are:

1. What do you want?

2. What have you been doing to get it?

3. Has what you have been doing worked?

4. What else could you do to get what you want?

5.   Are you ready to make a plan?

Each question corresponds to one of the benches in "A Walk in the Park." Let us consider each briefly and their role in assisting a worker to deal with their current challenge.

1.   What do you want? **Want Bench**

The Want Bench begins the journey through the M shaped path of the park. As we stated in Chapter Seven, every worker has a quality world or value system, which provides the motivation for his behaviors—the source of his wants. When a worker has a problem this means that, he perceives that some part of the real world does not match his quality world. In other words, he has a want that he does not know how to fill. Therefore, under every complaint, criticism, blame, or frustration is a want. It is important to help the worker put that want into words, which can provide an understanding and direction for his future actions. Therefore, this is the perfect place to start. It is common for this to be the first time that they have actually put what they want into specific words, since they are asked what they want, rather than, what they do not want. Of course, at all times in this journey the Lead Manager is careful to avoid any judgments of what the worker wants. This non-judgmental approach is crucial to the success of "A Walk in the Park."

2.   What have you been doing to get it? **Doing Bench**

The Doing Bench is the next bench to visit because it helps the worker to identify and appreciate all that they have been doing so far to deal with her challenge. It is often useful for the Lead Manager to have a way of recording or remembering each specific effort the worker has already made to solve her problem. This information has value later. For it is here that the Lead Manager can acknowledge all the efforts already made by the worker with out judging the appropriateness of any of them.

3.   Has what you have been doing worked? **Self-Evaluation Bench**

The Self-Evaluation Bench in the center of the park is next. This bench is in the center because it is crucial to the effectiveness of "A Walk in the Park." It is here that the worker gets to self-evaluate and let go of his earlier attempts to solve his problem while keeping his self-respect—a high value. It is here that the worker evaluates each of his earlier efforts. Since he self-evaluates without any judgment from his Lead Manager, he is able to let go of these choices and move on to find new options. This is the difference in the Lead Managed approach. We said earlier that workers learn best by self-evaluating their own work. This same principle applies here to their personal challenges outside of their work. Once a worker has self-evaluated his earlier behavior choices and heard himself, say they did not work, it becomes difficult, if not impossible, for him to use them again in the current situation. This then frees his creativity to generate other possible options at the next bench. If someone else evaluates his behaviors, he feels attacked and driven genetically to defend his actions in order to retain his self-respect or sense of power.

4.   What else could you do to get what you want? **Options Bench**

The Options Bench is next on the walk. Now the worker has freed himself from his ties to his earlier attempts because he has decided through self-evaluation that they were ineffective. He is ready to use his own creativity to identify other possible options to move him toward his quality world and values. Since the quality world is not real, the Lead Manager is striving, not to recreate the worker's quality world, but rather to move him towards some aspect of it that is deemed important. Again, it is important that the Lead Manager record or remember all the possible options that the worker generates. Strive for at least five to seven action options that he could take that would move him towards what he wants.

5.   Are you ready to make a plan? **Planning Bench**

At the Planning Bench, the worker selects one of his options from the previous bench that he believes will take him towards what he wants. It is vital that the choice be in the hands of the worker so that the result is also theirs, which will empower her. It is important for the Lead Manager to emphasize to the worker that, like all important things in life, her move toward what she wants will usually be achieved one small step at a time. The worker has selected the option. The Lead Manager then assists him or her to develop a specific and detailed plan of action that is likely to take them towards what they want by responding to the specifics of:

- *What* exactly are you going to do?
- *Who* specifically does it involve?
- *When* specifically are you going to do it?
- *Where* are you going to do it?
- *How* are you going to do it?

There is no need to ask why the worker will do the plan because the Lead Manager already knows that the *why* is because the worker perceives that it will take him toward his quality world or values. This approach is quick, simple and it works. Let us look at a few brief examples to illustrate:

At Jerri Inc., Gene approached Frank complaining that he cannot seem to focus on his work because he has discovered he has a heart condition including high blood pressure. He talks about all the frustrating efforts he has made to be healthier and about having a young family and being very worried about his future. Gene is one of Frank's longest serving employees and a model for many other staff in the organization. Frank asks Gene if he would like to talk about it for a few minutes—to take "A Walk in the Park." Gene agrees as Frank is not just his manager but also someone he trusts and respects. So let us follow their conversation to see and hear how Frank guides Gene through "A Walk in the Park."

Remember the five simple questions are:

1. What do you want?
2. What have you been doing to get it?
3. Has what you have been doing working?
4. What else could you do to get what you want?
5. Are you ready to make a plan?

1. Frank takes Gene first to the Want Bench—What do you want.

   Frank says: Gene that sounds scary to me, what do you want out of this situation you find yourself in right now?

   Gene responds: I want to have a future where I feel healthy and active. I want to continue to be able to work here; I enjoy my work. I want to be there for my family and continue to enjoy them. I want to see my kids grow up. I guess I want many things.

   Frank asks: Which one do you want first, want to move towards right away?

   Gene: Well I guess that would be getting my health back under control because everything else depends on that, doesn't it?

2. Frank takes Gene next to the Doing Bench—What have you been doing to get it?

   Frank: Gene, I think you are right! So what exactly have you been doing so far to get your health back under control?

   Gene: Well, let's see. I have been cutting back on the fast food, and I have been limiting my beer to a case a month. Also, I am trying to eat more chicken instead of beef and I am taking vitamins regularly.

3. Frank takes him next to the Self-Evaluation Bench—Has what you have been doing working?

   Frank says: Gene, you sound like you have been doing several things, but I want to ask you a question. Think about your answer carefully. Has cutting back on fast food and limiting the beer you drink, eating more chicken, and taking vitamins got you the control of your health you want?

   Gene: Well, they are supposed to help, and I have been doing them for months and they seem to work for other people ... but really ... when I think about it carefully they have not been enough to get me what I want.

4. Frank takes Gene next to the Options Bench—What else could you do to get what you want?

   Frank says: Gene, these behaviors may well work for others but I believe you are saying that they are not enough for you, is that right? (Gene nods) Then what else could you consider doing to take you towards having more control of your health?

Gene: Well, my doctor wants me to take blood pressure medication, and my wife wants me to cut out beer and beef all together. Also, I could do some exercising which I have avoided. And I guess I could take that stress management course that HR offers to us every year. And I could make more time for some of my hobbies like golf and fishing. When I think about it, more, many new options seem to appear.

5. Lastly, Frank takes him to the Planning Bench—Are you ready to make a plan?

    Frank says: Gene, you have created five new options that you could consider doing to move towards more control of your health. Which one appeals to you the most, and around which would you like to create an action plan?
    Gene: I would like to avoid medications if I can, and the stress management course scheduling is for next spring. I think the one that is most realistic for me at this point is the exercise option. I have been kind of putting if off knowing that eventually I would need to consider it. So, seize the opportunity, eh?
    Frank: Gene, what specifically are you prepared to do in terms of exercise that would take you towards more control of your health? And while we are at it, when, where and how are you going to do it; and who will it involve?
    Gene: I could start walking each evening after supper for twenty minutes around the neighborhood. And I could walk at a brisk pace to get my heart beating a little faster, but not too much. And maybe my wife or the kids will come with me sometimes.
    Frank: Gene, that sounds like a plan that will move you towards more control of your health. To ensure it's the right plan for you, would you self-evaluate it in terms of your commitment to doing it right away? On a scale of one to ten, with ten being the highest commitment, how strongly are you committed to it?"
    Gene: You know, Frank, just talking to you about it has helped me feel better and realize there are lots of things I can do to take better control of my health. My walking is a good first step for me, so I am really committed … at least an 8 or 9."
    Frank: That's great, Gene, I would be interested to know in a few days how it is going. Will you let me know?

Gene: I sure will Frank and thanks for listening I really appreciate it. I had better get back to work, eh?

Regardless of the nature of the problem, whether financial, family, drug abuse, personality conflicts, the process of guiding someone through "A Walk in the Park" does not change. Use the same path to the same benches in the same order.

Notice Frank's role as Lead Manager is to serve as a guide on the journey, asking the relevant questions in his own words. Frank does not punish, judge, criticize, blame, complain, anger, or threaten Gene. Frank knows, as a Lead Manager, that Gene will find the answers to his own challenges using his own creativity as long as Frank keeps him on the path to each bench in their prescribed order.

Using this approach will prove helpful in many work situations. To develop counseling skills, you will need some training in this area. Any organization that takes these ideas in this book seriously will offer its managers training in the counseling skills they need. An enlightening and enjoyable three-hour seminar enables anyone to learn this simple and effective "A Walk in The Park" approach. Trained faculty members of the William Glasser Institute are available for this purpose.

After experiencing bossing, many workers will be fearful of even admitting they have a problem, so initially the Lead Manager has to develop a way to encourage workers to bring problems to him, a statement of his approach. To do this, the manager has to state clearly from the beginning that he is only offering to help, not trying to blame or punish. What I suggest is that managers augment the sign previously suggested in Chapter 9 and post the following signed, comprehensive message in all departments:

My Approach
In any workplace, problems arise.
These may be between management and workers, among the workers, or just individual difficulties. Whatever they may be, if not solved to the satisfaction of all parties, we will be less able to produce quality products or render quality service, and our success as a company will suffer. We believe it is the manager's job to help solve problems, and we take this job seriously. We also believe that all problems have solutions without the use of threats or punishment from us or any of the parties involved. It is our goal to create a workplace where we care for each other and where you can be confident that we are doing all we can to make this a good place to work. When we do this, the company will prosper, and everyone will earn a fair wage.

After this sign goes up, it would be wise for the manager to gather the workers together to discuss what this sign means. The workers will tend to be skeptical, but if the manager conscientiously strives to practice what this sign advocates, a great deal of this skepticism will melt away. In addition, this sign will give the workers some idea of what is going on: the change from bossing to leading. People do not like mysteries, they incite fear, and Lead Managers make it their business to be open and above board in all they do.

Suppose a worker is chronically late for work. The manager needs to approach the worker and tell him that he thinks this is exactly the kind of problem he was referring to when he posted the sign. He could tell the worker that this could be a test of whether or not this new non-coercive approach will work. The worker will probably interrupt with an excuse or complaint about the company, because that is what bossed workers have always done to avoid blame or punishment.

Using the benches of "A Walk in the Park" as a guide, and with some give and take that I cannot exactly simulate, the manager needs to say, "I believe you want to get here on time (Want bench). I am not interested in excuses or complaints because I know you have been trying your hardest to get here on time (Doing Bench). I am also not interested in docking your wages or threatening you with the loss of your job. All I am interested in is how I can help you get here on time (Want Bench). I believe that if we talk for a few minutes, we can work this out (Self-Evaluation Bench). What do you suggest that we, each of us, both you and I, can do that will get you here on time (Options Bench & Planning Bench)?"

From this beginning, the manager and the worker would then talk and begin to solve the problem. After they have worked out a reasonable plan, the manager needs to say, "It is important that we talk again in a few days to see if what we have discussed is working. If you have solved the problem, I want to make sure that I know how you did it and what I did that helped. The more I know about how we solved this, the more I will be able to help another person with the same problem. In addition, I may want you to talk to another person with a similar problem and tell him how you solved it. Would you be willing to help me if that situation came up again?"

What is intended here is to get workers involved in helping each other solve small problems before they become too large. To do this, the Lead Manager shifts as many problems as possible to the workers themselves and acts as a teacher in the process.

This was an easy problem in that it would have been difficult for the worker to deny it existed. Other problems will not be so obvious. For example, you may have to deal with a worker who is a good producer but who is holding up production because he insists on doing more than he can physically accomplish in his section. Here the Lead Manager needs to emphasize the cornerstone of this counseling technique of asking the worker to evaluate his own work (Self-Evaluation Bench) as follows: "There seems to be a bottleneck here, and I want to see if we can fix it. You are working very hard, and you are doing good work. However, I want to talk to you about what seems to be a hold up and get your opinion on what we need to do to correct it. I can't solve this problem without some input from you."

Basic to non-coercive problem solving is to elicit the opinion or the judgment of the workers involved as to what they think the problem is. There is no threat here, only a genuine attempt to collect input as to what they think the problem is. If the manager gave it in the usual boss way, the workers would take it as criticism and resist. However, if the Lead Manager asks the workers first and listens carefully to what they have to say, it is likely the workers will then listen to him.

In this example, the worker may say the people who give him the work are giving it to him in such poor condition that he needs a lot of time to fix it. He claims he could work faster if they were doing their job, as they should. You might not agree, but you would not voice your disagreement. You could say he could be right, but it may take some time to get their work in better shape and the problem needs a solution quicker than this. You can then tell him you think he has too much to do, and, until he can take care of the incoming work, you want him to train a helper. You are not blaming or criticizing; you are offering him help, and he will probably be willing to accept it.

However, he may not be willing to do as you suggest, and you may have to take a different tack. The point is that you have opened up the problem to solution by getting him to evaluate his part, as well as the part of others, in solving it. It may take several more evaluations, but this is the non-coercive way to deal with problems.

The more success the manager has in creating the non-coercive, problem solving environment just discussed, the more likely it is that workers will bring problems to the manager. This is always better than the manager bringing up the problem, but the manager should not hesitate to bring them up. There is no need to wait for the workers to bring them to his attention. Once workers become aware of the fact that the manager is capable of helping them solve problems, whether he digs them up or they present them to him, the more the workers will be open to solving problems themselves, which is the ultimate goal of Lead Managing.

Whether we like it or not, everything that goes on in the workers' lives that might lead to imbalance or dissatisfaction has a potential detrimental effect on the quality of the work they do. Managers cannot do anything about the home lives of their workers, but if the Lead Manager provides the kind of work environment described so far, very few workers will take out their resentment of an unhappy home situation at work. This is one of the big plusses of Lead Management. Still, workers will have non-work-related problems that may eventually have a detrimental effect on their work. You should be prepared to offer "A Walk in the Park" to any worker with any problem as long as you feel comfortable dealing with that particular situation.

Most workers are used to talking about their problems, but they are not used to getting effective help with them. Most of the advice they get from friends and family reinforces what is usually their initial opinion: the problem is someone else's fault. They latch on quickly and strongly to that opinion. In fact, almost all of us do this because we do not want to take responsibility for what is not working out well in our lives. To take responsibility, we have to admit that we may have done something ineffective. We sense a loss of power, and, in a boss-managed workplace, we risk punishment. No one wants to lose power or experience punishment: it is too painful.

Workers with serious problems that are affecting the quality of their work rarely have anyone to turn to who knows how to counsel effectively. They tend not to want to go to a professional counselor, because to do so would be to admit inadequacy, which is the same as saying, "I am not as capable as I should be." This would not be a part of their value system. In addition, they mistakenly see counselors as professionals who treat crazy people and they, correctly, do not see themselves as crazy. They also fear that if they do go to a counselor, and a boss finds out about it, this will cost them something important such as a promotion. Moreover, to some extent this fear is rational. Unfortunately, all of this prevents people from getting the help they need.

Even if managers have training in some counseling skills, they still need to remember to only to counsel the people they manage as long as they feel they can offer help. They should be warned that if they feel uncomfortable they would be better off not to get involved. However, my experience in using the "A Walk in the Park" approach has proven to me that managers can handle most problems in the workplace simply and quickly. They need a small amount of training in the use of these concepts and this approach and the support to make the commitment to use it. Since workers with unsolved problems are a source of low-quality work, the pay-off in increased quality will far outweigh the small amount of time and money it takes to prepare managers for this important role.

Assuming the workers trust the Lead Managers, counseling workers who ask for help will usually be effective. The manager should make at least twenty to thirty minutes of uninterrupted time available and should ask the worker to explain the problem as best he can. Be patient and avoid interrupting while he is explaining what is bothering him.

For example, let us consider Jacqueline who, as an Assistant Director at the Millennium Community Hospital, complained to Marie that she does not have enough help to do the her job. She says, "There is just too much work!"

Marie arranges to meet with Jacqueline to take her for "A Walk in the Park." Marie suspects Jacqueline is not working efficiently; she is stuck in some old habits and needs to learn some new ways of doing things. After Jacqueline is finishes explaining the problem, Marie begins their journey through the park, let us follow them.

1. Marie takes her Jacqueline first to the Want Bench—What do you want?

    Marie says: Jacqueline, I appreciate your frustration, and, since our budget is tight, we need to use our ingenuity so we can solve this problem without anyone else's assistance. Let's start with you telling me what you want your job to be like right now?

    Jacqueline responds: I want to be on top of things, to be able to devote my time to the most important challenges in our section. We have the new seniors' service starting up next month. There are my continual recruitment duties, as well as, the ongoing financial and administrative stuff that I want under control.

    Marie asks: Which aspect is the most important to you right now and that you want to move towards immediately?

    Jacqueline: I would say that I want to feel a sense of control and balance with regard to all my responsibilities here at the hospital.

2. Marie takes her next to the Doing Bench—What have you been doing to get it?

    Marie: Jacqueline, what exactly have you been doing so far to get a sense of control and balance to your responsibilities?

    Jacqueline: Well, you know it is important that the new seniors' service starts strong. In addition, you cannot rely on just anyone to be as committed to it as I am. Most people do not have the experience and skills I have in recruitment so I have to do all that stuff myself as well. And, of course that new financial software we are using is complex and time consuming. Therefore, I have set aside Mondays and Tuesdays just for the new seniors' service. I have designated Wednesday mornings for finances, and I have scheduled all applicants' screenings for Thursday. And I left Fridays for the rest of my supervision duties, committee work, correspondence, and stuff like that.

3.   Marie takes her next to the Self-Evaluation Bench—Has what you have been doing working?

Marie says: Jacqueline, you obviously have implemented several changes, but I want to ask you an important question. Think about your answer carefully. Has setting aside Mondays and Tuesdays for the seniors' service and Wednesdays mornings for finances and Thursdays for applicants screening and Fridays for the rest of your duties got you the sense of control and balance to your responsibilities that you want? Jacqueline: Well, that's what I learned in that time management course I took last year and those techniques seem to work for Raymond and other people ... but actually ... when I look at it carefully they have not created, for me, a sense of balance or control in what I am doing.

4.   Marie takes her next to the Options Bench—What else could you do to get what you want?

Marie says: Jacqueline, these behaviors may well work for others, or even for you in other situations, but I think you just said that they are not for you in this situation. Is that right? (Jacqueline nods) Then what else could you consider doing to take you towards having more of a sense of balance and control in your job?

Jacqueline: Well, I am not sure. I have rather suspected that I need to delegate more things to others, but I am hesitant to do so for fear of looking incompetent. But when I hear myself say what I am doing isn't working, I realize that I may look that way already to some people. So I feel I have to do something different, don't I? It is important for me to continue with my team's supervision, but perhaps I could ask my administrative assistant to do more like some of the recruitment duties, or maybe I could make some time to take that familiarization course on the new software. I could also ask some of the committee members on the new seniors' service to take over some of the duties that I have been trying to do. And I also could learn to start saying no when someone wants to give me more work that I really don't have time to do. When I think about it there are more things that I can do than I realized.

5. Marie takes her lastly to the Planning Bench—Are you ready to make a plan?

    Marie says: Jacqueline you have identified four new behaviors that you could consider doing to move towards more balance and control of in your role here at the hospital. Which one do you think would start you on the road toward creating that balance and control you want? And, which you would like to build into an action plan?
    Jacqueline: I think my first step would be to deal with the most time consuming aspect, my recruitment responsibilities. That would probably make the biggest difference to me right now.
    Marie: Jacqueline, what specifically are you prepared to do in terms of your recruitment responsibilities that would take you toward more of a sense of balance and control in your job? And specifically when, where, and how are you going to do it; and who will it involve?
    Jacqueline: I plan to sit down with my administrative assistant, Shanti, a very skilled woman, and discuss all the tasks involved in my recruitment responsibilities and determine which ones she would be prepared to take on to free me up for other things. She has offered before to do more, but I have been hesitating. I will not do that anymore. I am going to book a time with her when I leave here, and we will sit down in my office over a cup of coffee. I will explain my situation and ask her for her assistance.
    Marie: That sounds like a plan that will move you towards more balance and control of your role. To ensure it is the best plan for you, would you self-evaluate it in terms of your commitment to doing it? On a scale of one to ten, with ten being the highest commitment, how strongly are you committed to it?
    Jacqueline: You know, Marie, having someone to listen to my concerns has added new perspectives that I just didn't notice before, and I feel better prepared to deal with it. In addition, I am noticing there are other things I will need to do but this is a great start. Thank you, this has been very helpful. So I am very committed ... a nine or ten."
    Marie: That's wonderful, Jacqueline. Can I call you next week to see how you are making out with it? And, of course, if you need to discuss

this again, I would be pleased to continue to assist you in this.

Jacqueline: Sure, Marie, and thank you, again. I really appreciate your time. I need to go book that appointment right now. I will talk to you next week.

As you can see, this is not very hard to do. Choice Theory®'s concept of assisting others to identify new behaviors that honor their values and move them toward what they want manifests itself throughout the process. In addition, what you want as a Lead Manager displays itself as well. It is far different from what a boss would do in that you do not step in with threats. Nor do you try to take over the problem and impose a solution that would antagonize the employee so much she would never consider your suggestion and might sabotage it to prove her point.

To repeat, I am not citing these examples to try to make you into a professional counselor. I know you have family and friends who you support all the time. What I am doing is showing you what you could do at work if you are willing to use a Lead Management counseling technique, "A Walk in the Park," and a few simple principles. This offer has the expectation that you will see it as something you could learn and use comfortably. The good part about this way to manage is that there is little risk. Even if you get into a problem that you realize is over your head, just admit that you are stumped and back away. As long as you do not promise any more than to sincerely help, it is unlikely you will cause any harm.

Let us consider Rose, one of the Team Leaders at Dave's Gas & Grocery who has a personal problem upsetting her effectiveness with her team. She tells Dave that her husband has left her, she is stuck with many bills and no support, and she is at her wit's end. Although she is normally a very good worker, she feels so alone and powerless that her work is not up to its usual standard.

Let's listen to Dave take Rose for "A Walk in the Park."

1. Dave takes Rose first to the Want Bench—What do you want?

    Dave says: Rose you are upset about this situation, and I appreciate you feeling overwhelmed about it all. Can we start with you telling me what you want out of this situation for yourself now?

    Rose responds: I want my husband back, I want help with our debt because I can't carry it all on my own, and I want to stop feeling so scared all the time.

Dave asks: Which one is the most important to you right now and that you want to move towards addressing immediately?

Rose: I would say that I want to stop feeling afraid all the time.

2.   Dave takes her next to the Doing Bench—What have you been doing to get it?

Dave: Rose, what exactly have you been doing so far to stop feeling afraid all the time?

Rose: Well, I have been calling him at his mother's place every night. I have written him a letter begging him to come home. I have asked his mother to help me get him back. I have asked my brother and two sisters to talk with him. I even went to his workplace to see if I could catch him at his lunch break to talk to him. I have also cleaned up the house and got in his favorite foods in case he decides to drop by to see me.

3.   Dave takes Rose next to the Self-Evaluation Bench—Has what you have been doing working?

Dave says: Rose, you obviously have initiated several actions to prevent you from feeling afraid, but I want to ask you a question. Think about your answer carefully. Has calling him, writing him letters, asking his mother or your brother and sisters to talk with him, or trying to talk to him yourself or having his favorite food handy enabled you to not feel afraid?

Rose: "Well, actually I think sometimes it is making it worse because he is avoiding me like the plague, and my family is getting frustrated with me too. One of my sisters said I was better off with him gone, but I feel so alone.

Dave: So Rose, let me ask you this question another way. The actions you took to reduce your fear of being scared, have they been successful for you?

Rose: Well when you say it that way and I think about it, I have to say no they have not. In fact, they almost increase my fear sometimes.

4.   Dave takes Rose next to the Options Bench—What else could you do to get what you want?

Dave says: Rose, these behaviors may well have worked for you in other situations in the past, but you just said that they are not working this time, it that correct. (Rose nods) Then what else could you consider doing to take you towards having less fear and more self-confidence in your life?

Rose: Well, I guess the opposite of being afraid is being self-confident isn't it? So if I want to feel more self-confident I could start doing things that give me a feeling of self-confidence like going out with my girl-friends to the craft courses, or I could spend more time with my own family who I know love me, or I could volunteer at the school where I would be welcome and appreciated. And I could put in more overtime to give me more money for the debts. Also, I could go back to school part time, so I am better prepared for a different future if he doesn't return. So, there are many things I can do to feel better.

5. Dave takes her lastly to the Planning Bench—Are you ready to make a plan?

Dave says: Rose you have identified five new actions that you could take to move you towards a feeling of less fear and more self-confidence in your life. Which one do you think would start you on the road toward creating that self-confidence you want, and which you would like to build into a specific plan of action for yourself?

Rose: I think I need to do them all, but the first one would be to talk to my own family about what has happened. I am so embarrassed, and yet I know they will be supportive and I need that right away.

Dave: Rose, what specifically are you prepared to do in terms of your own family to reduce your fear and increase your self-confidence? And specifically when, where, and how are you going to do it? And who will it actually involve?

Rose: I will call my parents tonight about going over for dinner on Sunday at their place. My brother and sisters are usually there. I will tell them all about my situation and ask them for their support regardless of whether he comes back or not.

Dave: Rose, that sounds like a plan that will move you towards more self-confidence and less fear in your life. To ensure it is the best plan for you at this time, would you self-evaluate it in terms of your commitment to doing it. On a scale of one to ten, with ten being the highest commitment, how strongly are you committed to it?

Rose: You know, Dave, having someone to bounce my situation off has given me a more objective perspective and challenged me to be stronger and value myself more. I feel stronger and more able to deal with it now.

In addition, I have learned that this is probably just the start of me evolving myself. I appreciate you not demeaning my situation or me. Thank you, this has been very useful. So I am at definite ten.
Dave: That's super Rose, will you let me know on Monday how it went with your family. And, if you need to talk about it again just drop by.
Rose: I will do that Dave. I will talk to you on Monday. Thanks again.

Dave may need to offer more assistance to Rose in the days ahead as she struggles to get control of her self and her emotions. However, the toughest part for both Dave and Rose is over because she has started to take control of her life again. In addition, at the same time, Dave has retained a valuable employee.

With many of the people you help, it is not so much that you can do something specific as you can help them appreciate that no matter how bleak things seem, they can help themselves and, by being there, you assist them in finding the strength to make the effort. By listening to them respectfully without judgment, you honor their Hierarchy of Being, which encourages them to follow it. Even if you do not think you do much, what I suggest here is usually so much more than they have available to them; what seems little to you can be a great deal to them.

Finally, let us look at one more difficult problem. You know that a key worker is drinking or using mind altering drugs off the job and maybe, a little at work, but he is too clever for you to catch him and I advise you not to try. If you catch him, you may end up being coercive or threatening, which would be counterproductive. If you are sure of the facts, and you usually are, you need to confront him with the problem. How you do this is crucial.

Alcohol and certain other drugs impair the human perceptual system. As a result, it is often difficult for those taking them to make accurate self-evaluations. Because of this, you need to be more firm and directive than in other situations. With an alcohol or drug problem, the worker often feels coerced, especially by his or her manager. This is because in order to do your job as a Lead Manager you will need to remind the drugged worker that if he chooses to continue using the drugs he is are also choosing not to work for you. Therefore, it is important to be very matter-of-fact, as if there is nothing else you can do except confront him with his drug abuse. The worker may accuse you of coercion, and he or she is right in the sense that they may think you are forcing them into a decision corner. However, this is about the best you can do with drinkers who have altered perceptual systems.

Tell him you believe he has a drinking problem, and it is causing his work to suffer. If he denies it, as he likely will, tell him you expected him to deny it, but his denial is not going to make you change your mind. Explain that from your knowledge of drug abuse, he has to stop or his work will deteriorate further, and he will not be able to stop unless he gets involved with a group like Alcoholic Anonymous that has a good record of accomplishment for helping people like him stop using. Finally, tell him you are willing to help, but there is not too much more you can do. It is up to him to take the first step and visit a program. The local alcohol foundation has lists of places where he can seek help. You may need to get a copy of this list and give it to him.

Tell him you want to talk to him tomorrow, but today, even if it is in the middle of a shift, send him home. This way he knows you are serious. You will not have anyone you are managing remain at work if there is even the slightest possibility of impairment. It could endanger others. Tell him to come in early tomorrow to see you and tell you his plan. If your company and union rules allow, tell him not to go back to work until he has written and signed a plan, and it must start tomorrow, no later.

If he says you are too hard, that you have no proof he even has a drinking problem, say this is all you will do. Anything less will not work and you care too much about him and his capacity to do a good job to do anything else.

You will, however, listen to him tomorrow even though you know he will not come up with anything better, because what you are offering is all there is. Addiction is a special problem that does not lend itself to counseling until the addict has actually stopped using the alcohol or other drugs. If you are not firm, he has little chance to regain control of his life. Once he is involved in a good plan, do not say anything more about his drinking. Any conversation about drinking and drugs is usually counterproductive in that he may see the discussion as a softening on your part, think you are not serious, and use this as an excuse to drink again. Avoid this trap.

Any manager who wants to learn to counsel as suggested in this chapter needs to do more than read this book. For further information on how to learn more about everything in this book, contact the author or the William Glasser Institute.

Seven Key Chapter Points

1. Telling a worker what to do appears coercive, so, instead, Lead Managers use an asking approach.

2. Using Lead Management demands that we listen as much as we talk to workers.

3. Workers require fair treatment in all areas so expectations must apply to all.

4. Lead Managers do not give up on problems but take a we can do it approach to all challenges presented.

5. Lead Managers deal with problems as they arise and are willing to listen and counsel workers if they are interested.

6. Tools like "A Walk in the Park" assist workers in dealing with problems inside and outside of work.

7. Lead Managers also know when to refer their workers to outside professional help.

A Quality Conclusion

At a Community Business Social, Dave, Frank, and Marie were talking about the main challenge they each face on a daily basis:

If you look around, you cannot help but see that poor quality products and services pervade every part of society. To survive and compete successfully, every organization, whether private or public, needs to produce more quality. The global economy magnifies this need. In addition, the evolving demographics in industrialized economies, which indicate that there are pending shortages of workers in most sectors of our economy, aggravates the situation even more. These shortages have already begun to appear in many sectors including carpenters, nurses, educators, and plumbers.

We may lament what various governments have done that challenges efforts to achieve quality: tax breaks for hostile takeovers that lead to the looting of viable companies or the free markets offered to all no matter how they treat their workers. This is not my specific area of expertise nor can much alter these factors in the short term. What I do know is that if we do not improve the ways we manage the people who do the work in both profit and non-profit organizations, working on other needed changes will be ineffective anyway.

Intent is critical here. Organizations need to focus their attentions, on purpose, on the main way they can remain viable by producing the finest products and services available anywhere. They need to be not just a little better, but significantly better and less costly than what others are able to produce. Organizations will be able to do this if managers make the effort, on purpose, to conceptualize a quality workplace and then put that conception into their own quality world, on purpose. This purposeful intention is the first and continuing task of a Lead Manager.

The organizations that are in trouble are in that state primarily because their employees are expected to produce twenty-first century products and services while being managed with nineteenth and twentieth century approaches. It will not work because we have evolved our understanding of individuals, organizations, and society. What is required is a Lead Management approach that respects this awareness.

We need to move beyond dysfunctional Boss Management, whose time has come and gone. This new century requires an approach that treats people as individuals who operate at a level of heightened awareness of their values and dreams—an approach that gets workers to giver an organization their energy, creativity, and commitment and an approach that ensures the workers experience both respect and value in their workplace. Moreover, it needs to occur intentionally—on purpose.

So let us consider an evolved Snow White …

THE STORY OF A LEAD MANAGER

Once upon a time, in a far away kingdom, there lived a beautiful princess named Snow White. Like many people of royal blood down through the ages, she was wise beyond her years. Having grown up the daughter of a king and queen and having watched them rule their realm with respect, caring, and trust, she felt she had learned many useful things about leadership.

Being an enterprising young woman, one day Snow White left the security of her parent's kingdom to seek her fortune in the big, wide world. She traveled for many days and looked in many places for an opportunity to make her mark on the world. One day she came across an enterprise that she thought was ideal for her. It was a small diamond mine with only seven employees. One of them, called Doc, oversaw its operation. Doc cared about his workers, but they did not believe it because of some of the policies and procedures he had instituted and the way he implemented them. Doc tended to be impatient with them and was prone to punishing them with extra work or threatening them with layoff. Other times he even tried coercing them with free trips to Disneyland for meeting production quotas.

As a result, there was dissatisfaction among the workers; they felt unappreciated and distrustful of their boss-manager. One worker, Grumpy, experienced so much frustration that he was avoided by his fellow workers. Another, Sneezy, was absent on sick leave a lot while Dopey was suspected of using drugs in the mine. Happy, on the other hand, did just enough to collect his pay while focusing on his outside work he called his hobbies—sports. Sleepy sought out remote locations in the mine to take frequent, unscheduled breaks. Finally, Bashful felt so unchallenged at his job that he was thinking of seeking employment elsewhere, possibly in the IT industry. The team seemed to lack consistency in the volume and quality of their product and was often distracted from the task by spontaneous breaks and bouts of singing and dancing in the mine.

While the mine had been around for a while, the operation was finding it more and more difficult to hold its own in the highly competitive global diamond industry. Snow White felt that these workers wanted to produce high quality diamonds. However, outdated leadership hampered their intentions. Threatening their competitive edge further was the emergence of foreigners in their industry. In fact, Canadians had opened two mines in the north and had begun the practice of labeling each of their diamonds with an engraved polar bear as their signature of their commitment to quality.

Underneath this façade of frivolity in the mining operation, Snow White could see that the workers were skilled people. They had a vast store of expertise that she needed to lead and support to make the mining operation profitable. Yet Snow White felt they lacked both the sound leadership and good management practices to be successful. She knew that they could produce not only more product but also product of a much higher quality to compete more favorably if only they had a Lead Manager. Having watched her parents lead a country, she felt confident she could lead the staff to dramatically improve the mine's bottom line.

All seven dwarfs were impressed with Snow White's trust in their abilities, her caring for their future well-being, and her respect for them as people. They also liked her commitment to listening to their concerns and how she said they could always improve their product if they worked together. Therefore, they all agreed, Doc somewhat reluctantly, to let her Lead Manage their operation so that they could improve the quality and quantity of their diamond production.

Snow White began immediately to hold individual meetings with each team member listening to their goals and recording what they thought would improve the operation. She asked each member to start evaluating their own work and look for ways to improve it. She also instituted regular team meetings so they also could set production goals based on the latest data they had available on the operation.

She did not waste time blaming, criticizing, threatening, or coercing her team but instead implemented an open door policy whereby anyone who was seeking a problem-solving strategy was welcome at her door. She called it "A Walk in the Park," and impressed the team with both its simplicity and effectiveness. Eventually they began using it with each other and then with themselves both inside and outside work.

The dwarfs noticed the difference right away. It began with each of them feeling more valued at work because someone was actually listening to them, acting on their input, and trusting them to use their genius to do a quality job. Of course, the team began to work more closely together and depend on each other more. Doc was the first to comment on the changing atmosphere in the mine. One day he asked Snow White if she had noticed that Sneezy's absenteeism had dropped dramatically. Grumpy eventually volunteered to head up the social committee and developed a reputation for throwing the best parties around. Dopey eventually entered a drug rehabilitation program for which he credits his eventual promotion to safety committee chair. Happy brought his focus back to work and channeled some of it into coaching the company hockey team using the Lead Management principles he had learned. Sleepy, with his new role as customer service representative, kept busy generating new clients for the mine. Moreover, Bashful did not leave the mine, and instead became Snow White's executive assistant. He still turns beet red when she says to others that he is a genius and one of the keys to the mine's success.

Some say the seven dwarfs were lucky that Snow White came along. They say she knew the real business world of today. Snow White contends that it was their team, which made the difference in their success. She commented recently, "It was the intentional effort of all of us working together, with respect, caring, and commitment which has made us the Fortune 500 companies we are today."

You can still hear their song echoing across the mine, but its lyrics have evolved to:

Hi ho, hi ho, it is off to work we go,
Hi ho, hi ho, we are making lots of dough,
Hi ho, hi ho, quality is our aim,
Hi ho, hi ho teamwork is our game.

Afterword

Having read through *Using Lead Management on Purpose!*, you now have a greater sense of what the difference is between successful and unsuccessful organizations. You probably reminded yourself of what you already knew at some level of your own Hierarchy of Being: that people only offer their genius to their employer when they perceive they are valued and respected for who they are at all levels of their being. In addition, it is this value and respect, conveyed regularly in a form the worker recognizes, which enables an organization to manifest its purpose and mission.

The challenge now becomes how to translate *Using Lead Management on Purpose!* into actions within your own organization. Be forewarned that you will meet skeptics who doubt that Lead Management will make a difference. However, you will know from your own learning and experiences that it will. Your certainty will be repeatedly tested; be ready for it and welcome it as an opportunity to offer insight and evolution to another person on the same journey as the rest of us.

Finally, remember that when we change our perceptions, we breed changed perceptions in others. It is the way of nature and evolution. So focus on your own evolution and observe what occurs. It will make for an interesting and exciting future for you and your organization.

Glossary

Acting/doing: One of the four parts of every behavior that entails the actions of our body at a specific moment in time

Behavior: The four-part process of what we do and think which then generates a feeling and a physiological response

Belief: A generalized perspective that we have learned because of a collection or one or more experiences

Belief system: A set of generalized perspectives that summarize the significant life experiences

Boss management: An approach to communicating emphasizing an authority differential and ignoring the needs and values of others

Choice Theory®: An approach to communication emphasizing a balance of authority while respecting the need and values of others

Criticism: An approach to communication that looks at only the negative side of a situation

Careful Communication: An approach to communication wherein one person ignores his or her own values and gives priority to the values of the other person

Careless communication: An approach to communication wherein one person asserts their values are the right ones and the other person's are not important

Caring communication: An approach to communication wherein one person respects their own values and that of the other person and so inserts their values inside that of the other person to create clearer communication

Coach: An individual who offers information and other perspectives to someone who has requested it

Counselor: An individual who supports and challenges an individual or group to learn to believe in his or her own potential

External Control Psychology: A belief system that holds that people are motivated primarily by rewards and punishments from the world outside them

Feeling: One of four parts of human behavior that is generated by what the person is doing with their body and thinking with their mind at that moment in time

Friend: A person who has your welfare in mind when he or she makes a decision

Freedom: The genetically encoded need to make the important decisions in one's life

Hierarchy of Being: A description of the five levels of awareness in which humans can think about themselves

Identity: A level of the Hierarchy of Being and refers to a person's perception of who they are as a person

Lead Management: An approach to business leadership and management that emphasizes communicating with workers at all levels of their being in the pursuit of excellent products and services for a global economy

Lead Manager: An individual who communicates at all levels of the workers' being in the pursuit of excellent products and services for a global economy

Leadership: The art and skill of seeing and drawing out the genius in every worker in the pursuit of common goals

Leader: An individual who operates at all levels of his or her own being and that of the people with whom he or she interacts in the pursuit of his or her own evolution

Love: The act of recognizing the symmetry of every aspect of life

Manager: The person responsible for consistency of purpose and continuity in an organization

Need: A genetic requirement for the continued life of an organism

Power: A genetically encoded need to feel listened to, to have influence on others, and to make a difference in one's own life.

Physiology: One of the four parts of behavior that reflects the internal bodily changes that occur generated by what the person is doing and thinking at that moment in time

Perception: The interpretation an individual makes of sensory information based on his or her belief system

Quality: Those perceptions an individual makes that tie closely to his or her highest beliefs and values

Quality World: An imagined collection of sensory information that individuals create over their life to reflect their highest beliefs and values

Quality Product: A product that enough people put into their quality world to make it profitable to produce

Quality Service: A service that enough people put into their quality world to make it profitable to provide

Role-Clarification Matrix: A tool that used to clarify roles between two individuals who work together in an organization

Spirit: The highest level of the Hierarchy of Being; a person's perception of how he or she connects to the universe and its laws

Strategies: A level of the Hierarchy of Being reflecting a person's creative thinking used to manifest his or her beliefs and values.

Seven Caring Choice Theory® habits: The seven behaviors that foster communication between people: accepting, respecting, trusting, encouraging, supporting, listening, and negotiating.

Seven Deadly Habits: The seven behaviors that do not foster communication between people: criticizing, blaming, threatening, bribing, punishing, complaining, and nagging.

Thinking: One of the four parts of behavior that refer to the two levels of thought that occurs within a person at a given moment of time, specifically the associated thoughts about the situation and the disassociated thoughts about the self, being in the situation.

Value: Anything that a person has come, through his or her life experiences, to believe will lead him or her toward pleasure and away from pain.

Worker: An individual hired to bring energy, creativity, and commitment to a goal.

Resources

The
Using Lead Management on Purpose!
<u>Seminar</u>

Avoid these organizational minefields ...

Low Quality Work! * Poor Service! * Problem Employees!
Dissatisfied Customers! * Failing Bottom Line!
Learn to produce Excellent Products or Services
With Creative, Energized, and Committed Employees
Who Foster Customer Loyalty!

Ken uses cutting-edge psychology and accelerated-learning
techniques in this three-hour seminar that guarantees:
1. You will *receive* 7 **Lead Management Tools** to apply now!
2. You will *become* **the Leader your team trusts and works for
diligently**!
3. You will *have* **the satisfaction of knowing and practicing
the Lead Management secrets** that produce quality products
or services!
Take the Next Step ... and
Book This Seminar for You and Your Team!
Group Rates Apply—Call Today!
Call Toll Free 1-877-569-3710
ken@clarendonconsulting.com
Info: www.usingleadmanagementonpurpose.com
www.clarendonconsulting.com

The following is a list of resource web sites that are available to explore the ideas, techniques, and tools mentioned in *Using Lead Management on Purpose!*

Clarendon Consulting
Kenneth L. Pierce
44 Grafton St.
Charlottetown, PE
C1A 1K5 Canada
Phone: 1-902-569-3710
Toll Free: 1-877-569-3710
Fax: 1-902-569-5433
Email: ken@clarendonconsulting.com
Web site: www.clarendonconsulting.com

The William Glasser Institute,
22024 Lassen Street, Suite 118,
Chatsworth, CA 91311 USA
Phone: 1-800-899-0688
Toll Free: 1-818-700-8000;
Fax: 1-818-700-0555;
Email: wginst@wglasser.com
Web site: wglasser.com

The Concourse of Wisdom School, Houston Texas
2800 Post Oak Blvd, Suite 5250
Houston, TX 77056 USA
Phone: 1-713-850-1234
Toll Free: 1-888-DEMARTINI
Fax: 1-713-850-9239
Email: info@drdemartini.com
Web site: www.drdemartini.com

Works Cited

Aguayo, Rafael. *Dr. Deming: The American Who Taught the Japanese about Quality.* New York New York: Fireside. 1991.

Abraham, Carolyn. *Possessing Genius: The Bizarre Odyssey of Einstein's Brain.* New York, New York: St. Martin's Press. 2001.

Bennis, Warren. *On Becoming a Leader.* Boston Massachusetts: Addison-Wesley Publishing Company. 1995.

Bennis, Warren and Biederman, Patricia Ward. *Organizing Genius The Secret of Creative Collaboration.* Boston Massachusetts: Addison-Wesley Publishing Company. 1997.

Bridges, Scott. *Motivating Factors.* Effect Magazine, Fall, 2006.

Demartini, John. *The Heart of Love: How to Go Beyond Fantasy to Find True Relationship Fulfillment.* Carlsbad California: Hay House. 2007.

Dilts, Robert B., Epstein, Todd and Dilts, Robert W. *Tools for Dreamers Strategies for Creativity and the Structure of Innovation Creativity and the Structure of Innovation,* Cupertino California: Meta Publications. 1991.

Emerson, Ralph Waldo. *Essays and English Traits.* New York New York: P. F. Collier & Sons Corporation.1969.

Gabor, Andrea. *The Man Who Discovered Quality.* Toronto Ontario: Random House of Canada Limited. 1990.

Glasser, William. *The Quality School: Managing Students Without Coercion.* New York New York: Perennial Library. 1990.

Glasser, William. *The Quality School Teacher.* New York New York: Harper Perennial. 1993.

Glasser, William. *The Control Theory Manager*. New York New York: Harper Perennial. 1994.

Glasser, William. *Choice Theory®: A New Psychology of Personal Freedom*. New York New York: Harper Collins. 1998.

Glasser, William. *For Parents and Teenagers—Dissolving the Barrier Between You And Your Teen*. New York New York: Harper Collins. 2003.

Leatherman, D. *Quality Leadership through Empowerment*. Amherst Massachusetts: HRD Press, Inc. 1992.

Martin, William B. *Quality Customer Service*. Menlo Park California: Crisp Publications, Inc. 1989.

Senge, Peter M., Kleiner, Art., Roberts, Charlotte, Ross, Richard B., Smith, Bryan J. *The Fifth Discipline Fieldbook Strategies and tools for Building a Learning Organization*. New York New York: Currency Doubleday dell Publishing Group Inc. 1994.

Townsend, Patrick L. and Gebhardt, Joan. *Quality in Action*. New York New York: John Wiley & Sons Inc.1992.

Vance, Mike and Deacon, Diane. *Break Out of the Box*. New Jersey: Career Press. 1996.

Wellins, Richard S., Byham, William C. and Wilson, Jeanne M. *Empowered Team*, San Francisco California: Jossey-Bass Inc. 1991.

Endnotes

[1] Dilts, Epstein and Dilts, "Tools for Dreamers Strategies for Creativity and the Structure of Innovation," 26.

[2] Emerson, "Essays and English Traits," 60.

[3] Demartini, "The Heart of Love," 41.

[4] Bennis, "On Becoming a Leader," xiii.

[5] Abraham, "Possessing Genius—The Bizarre Odyssey of Einstein's Brain," 308-342.

[6] Bennis and Biederman, "Organizing Genius The Secrets of Creative Collaboration," 211.

[7] Bennis, "On Becoming a Leader," xiii.

[8] Bennis and Biederman, "Organizing Genius The Secrets of Creative Collaboration," 199.

[9] Townsend and Gebhardt, "Quality in Action," 244.

[10] Aguayo, "Dr. Deming: The American Who Taught the Japanese About Quality," 141.

[11] Bennis, "On Becoming a Leader," xiii.

[12] Townsend and Gebhardt, "Quality in Action," 245.

[13] Townsend and Gebhardt, "Quality in Action," 241.

[14] Bridges, "Motivating Factors," 3.

[15] Demartini, "The Heart of Love," 40.

[16] Demartini, "The Heart of Love," 41.

[17] Wellins, Byham and Wilson, "Empowered Teams," 129.

[18] Senge et al., "The Fifth Discipline Fieldbook Strategies and Tools for Building a Learning Organization," 51.

About the Author

Ken Pierce, a board-certified psychologist, has worked for thirty years in corporate training, psychology, and education. Ken is an international speaker, author, holds Senior Faculty status in the William Glasser Institute of Los Angles, and is an adjunct professor in psychology at the University of Prince Edward Island. He is a Certified Trainer in DACUM Occupational Analysis and Neuro-Linguistic Programming. As well, he holds a Learning Management Diploma in Competency Based Education from Holland College and is Certified by the Demartini Human Research and Education Foundation, Houston Texas.

Ken has published in the areas of occupational analysis, stress management, and learning environments and is currently working on an publication on schoolyard bullying. Ken, known nationally and internationally for his work, facilitates in his several areas of expertise. Ken has conducted numerous keynotes and seminars on organizational change, Lead Management, education, psychology, and related topics. Ken lives with his wife, Anna, in Stratford, Prince Edward Island, where he consults, teaches, and writes.

Index

The letter *f* following a page number denotes a figure.

978-0-595-44832-6
0-595-44832-1

www.ingramcontent.com/pod-product-compliance
Lightning Source LLC
Chambersburg PA
CBHW030740180526
45163CB00003B/864